PIN ACTION

PIN ACTION

SMALL-TIME GANGSTERS, HIGH-STAKES GAMBLING, AND THE TEENAGE HUSTLER WHO BECAME A BOWLING CHAMPION

GIANMARC MANZIONE

PEGASUS BOOKS
NEW YORK LONDON

PIN ACTION

Pegasus Books LLC
80 Broad Street, 5th Floor
New York, NY 10004

Copyright © 2014 by Gianmarc Manzione

First Pegasus Books edition December 2014

Interior design by Maria Fernandez

Grateful acknowledgment is made to Luby Publishing, the United States Bowling Congress, the Professional Bowlers Association, Cathy and Ernie Schlegel, Steve Harris, Kenny Barber, and Frans Evenhuis for providing the photos and illustrations that appear in this book.

Library of Congress Cataloging-in-Publication Data is available.

ISBN: 978-1-60598-645-6

10 9 8 7 6 5 4 3 2 1

Printed in the United States of America
Distributed by W. W. Norton & Company

In memory of John Mazzio and Kenny Barber

CONTENTS

PREFACE

Some people ask me how a guy with an MFA in poetry ended up writing a book about bowling alleys full of gambling gangsters. I have never found an adequate explanation for that divorce between the two poles of my existence—one, the kid who squandered his childhood in the bowling alleys of Brooklyn; the other, the college student who fell in love with books as his bowling balls gathered dust in his dad's garage.

No experience heightened that discordancy more than the writing of this book. Particularly toward the end, while I was teaching English and creative writing at College of Central Florida, one night I would be studying spondaic substitution in "Fra Lippo Lippi" and the next I would be banging away at stories about gamblers and gangsters who troubled the bowling alleys of Brooklyn and beyond.

When I was a student at Manhattan College, I used to bowl Monday night leagues in Brooklyn at Maple Lanes on the corner of 60th Street and 16th Ave., a place made famous by legendary action bowlers such as Richie Hornreich long before

I came into this world. I used to take a book with me and read between shots, usually new volumes of poems by contemporary poets such as Philip Levine or Denise Levertov. After I bowled a 300 game there on November 13, 2000, some of the guys I bowled with told me maybe they would start reading, too. Look what it was doing for me!

Then they did what guys did for so many action bowlers back in the day—they gave me a moniker. Mine was "Shakespeare"—you know, the Michael Jordan of books. I myself was no action bowler—by 2000, action bowling as it was known in the 1960s had faded into an obscure collection of characters and stories—but this tradition of giving names that represented what made guys tick was one that still held strong in the Brooklyn alleys. "Shakespeare" was not bad, but it also was not nearly as interesting as some of the monikers attributed to those who roamed the underworld that was 1960s action bowling—names like One Finger Benny, Tony Sideweight, Bernie Bananas, and so many more.

Maple Lanes was closed down in 2013 to be replaced by apartment buildings and a synagogue. In 2006, Leemark Lanes on 88th Street between 4th Ave. and 5th Ave. closed down to be replaced by a six-story parking structure for customers of Century 21, one of many retailers on 86th Street whose revolving doors and sales signs distinguish one of the busiest shopping districts in Bay Ridge. Leemark was a place where many wise old men taught me as much about bowling as they taught me about life; to see it vanish was a crushing blow for me and for the many people who also made cherished memories there over the years. The list of bowling alleys that once speckled the five boroughs but are no longer standing easily could fill at least a full page or two of this book. And that is the reason I wanted to write it. *Pin Action* is an attempt to hold time still, to stop it from turning the way things are into the way things were.

Today, throughout New York City, bowling tends to be a trendy afterthought in night clubs that just happen to have bowling lanes in them, places where 20-somethings are as likely to go for a Cosmo as they are to go for a pair of funny-looking shoes. Establishments like The Gutter or Brooklyn Bowl in Williamsburg, or Bowlmor Lanes inside the old New York Times building in Times Square, are jettisoning bowling into a glittery new era where the sport once ruled by Don Carter and Dick Weber now is ruled by celebrity chefs and craft cocktails. *Pin Action* memorializes the world where you kept score by hand, an all-night match left you with a bloated and bleeding bowler's thumb by sunrise, and a combination of tobacco and lane oil smudged your calloused fingertips.

That is the world I began to learn about when I spent long afternoons listening to the avuncular and salty-haired regulars at Leemark and Maple talk about the old days. I was 11 years old at the time. The guys would tell me, for instance, about a bowling alley that once existed down a stairway accessible from the Fortway Theatre in Dyker Heights, how that was where Brooklyn's own Johnny Petraglia, one of the sport's overarching legends, started turning the heads of sharks and shysters with his talent at age 14. By the time I was growing up near Dyker Heights, that place next to the theatre where Petraglia once made waves was a gun range, its historical significance in sports history completely effaced. The theatre itself, where I had gone to see many movies with my cinephile father over the years, closed down in 2005. A Chinese supermarket took its place in 2007.

Names other than Petraglia's would find their way into the stories I heard at Leemark and Maple. Names like Richie Hornreich, Mike Limongello, Mark Roth, Ernie Schlegel, Mike Chiuchiolo, Kenny Barber, Ira "The Whale" Katz, Hank Burrough, Dirty Willie, Frank Medici, Psycho Dave, and so many others. It all sounded like some page torn out of a Jimmy Breslin book. But this was real; these were real people, real lives, and they had passed through the very place where I first got acquainted with the sport of bowling in the distant aftermath of so much sordid history.

I could tell from the looks in the eyes of those who told me about these characters and their stories that there was a lot more to those guys than a name. In pro shops around town I gazed in awe at memorabilia like bowling balls with Mark Roth's signature on them as if I had discovered the signature of God. I still was too young to really understand why I felt that way back then; I only had the impression that something very big had happened there long before I came around. The more time went on the more I wanted to know about it. And the more bowling drifted into the background of my blooming love affair with literature and writing as I got older, the more I realized I was developing an ability to communicate my passion for the subculture into which my childhood immersed me. *Pin Action* is the culmination of that discovery.

As the stories that had absorbed me back when I was a kid listening to the old guys at Brooklyn bowling alleys lingered with me over the years, I developed an insatiable desire to know more about the New York City my parents and grandparents knew. I wanted to know about what things were like back before the 802 Club on 64th Street and 8th Ave. in Brooklyn—where *Saturday Night Fever* was filmed—became a medical building. I wanted to know more about the New York where Melody Lanes in Sunset Park was not yet the only place in southwest Brooklyn where you could bring the kids for a few games of bowling on a Sunday afternoon. What was it like when bowling alleys were as plentiful in New York City as the newsstands (remember those?).

I started asking around, beginning with my parents, and, much later, the action bowlers, whose stories I tell in this book. The things they told me gave me a glimpse of the way things were, just as the old guys at Leemark and Maple had back in my childhood, and I was hooked. This book started storming within me, and I felt as though I never would forgive myself if I failed to let it out.

I once asked former action bowler Red Bassett, for instance, about the 802 Club.

"When we were kids hanging out in Bay Ridge, we would sneak into the 802," he told me. "The owner would see us and scream at us and kick us out. But after Johnny did a lot of good things on tour, oh, now they couldn't get enough of us! Then we were something, ya know, and I just went along."

Memories like that one are scraps of an irretrievable past I tried to salvage here in the pages of *Pin Action*. Bassett and so many others left pieces of themselves somewhere back in the bygone world that colors the pages of this book; I only hope I have done at least some justice to the time and place they knew. And so, reader, welcome back to the past. If it is even remotely as much fun for you to read about as it was for me to write about, then the journey will have been well worth the trip for both of us.

1
A FISH IN PHILADELPHIA

The first time eighteen-year-old Ernie Schlegel and his posse stepped inside Jimmy Dykes Lanes looking for action, the name of the place itself should have been their first clue about the kind of night they were in for. A famed ballplayer-turned-manager for the Philadelphia Athletics, Dykes was a hardscrabble Philly kid whose wrists grew as strong as a bull's legs from working as a pipe fitter. As a manager, he spewed such venom at umpires over balls and strikes that fans were almost as likely to witness his ejection as they were to witness a ground-out to short.

But on this particular night it wasn't just the streets of Philadelphia and their assorted characters that Schlegel and the boys faced; it was a part of town down on Route 1 in south Jersey that they knew better than to visit again by the time the night was through. They knew better than to do a lot of things by then. They knew to call it quits when they were ahead. They knew not to take small-time bets from gamblers who will mug you at knifepoint if they lose. And they knew you only humiliate a man in his own house if you have enough weapons to make it out alive.

Such were the lessons you learned late at night in the bowling alleys of Philly and south Jersey in 1962, places Schlegel prowled in the back of Toru Nagai's slick black Cadillac with his enterprising sidekick, Steve Harris, in tow. Nagai, a diminutive Japanese restaurateur who ran a sandwich shop near Columbia University, chauffeured Schlegel to big-money matches out of state on weekends like a horse breeder cashing in on his prized pony. Harris, twenty, was a street-wise Jewish kid with horn-rimmed glasses who grew up on the same tough streets as Schlegel. When he still lived with his parents, his mother threatened to lock him out of the house if he kept coming home in the middle of the night. Harris, who never turned down a chance to bet on Schlegel whenever he hit the lanes, went out anyway. He once came home to find the chain of his mother's apartment door locked, his mother standing on the other side lambasting him for being a hoodlum and refusing to open the door. Harris went back out into the streets and rode the subway the rest of the night.

Harris made an uninspired attempt at the life of a nine-to-fiver by picking up odd jobs as a mail boy for the Baumritter furniture company, which later became Ethan Allen; working for his father as an exterminator; trying and failing to complete classes at New York University and The City University of New York. Harris had little interest in college. He grew up boarding buses with his buddies and heading off to Newark to see the stripper Tempest Storm perform at Minsky's Burlesque at age 16. They once caught her bra in the crowd. The Minsky's in Times Square had been closed down in 1942 by Mayor La Guardia, but no amount of distance was great enough to keep

Harris and his friends from doing what had to be done to tell their friends they had gotten their hands on Tempest Storm's bra. The Minsky's Harris and his buddies knew in 1956 was a place that mingled comedians with strippers while guys sold candy in the aisles between acts as a band played. Later, when Harris's parents gave him $250 to register for those classes at CUNY, he took it to the horse track in Yonkers and blew it all. He then put on a farce that lasted for months: He gathered a bundle of books each morning in conspicuous view of his parents and headed out—seemingly to school. They had no idea their money had gone to the ponies, or that the "school" he learned in had little to do with books but everything to do with life. It was a school Harris attended in the poker rooms, horse tracks, bowling alleys and goulash houses of New York City.

Schlegel, for his part, did pick up a job for $48 a week at the Benrus Watch Company store where his mother worked as a clerk. One day, he fell asleep standing up, about eight weeks into the gig, and that was the last time he tried to squeeze a round peg into the square hole of the lives his parents lived. Schlegel knew as well as Harris that the real money was made in the bowling alleys out in Jersey or somewhere in Brooklyn or the Bronx, where he pulled in the cash he would later stuff in his sock drawer at home. He had some explaining to do the day his mother found that stockpile of cash while putting away his clothes. That was the day she realized her son already had a job, and it had nothing to do with selling watches. He persuaded her that you don't always need to pull a menial paycheck working hours in a factory to get by. The smart ones made their own hours and called nobody "boss." Schlegel was one of the smart ones, he insisted. The point was not that kids like Schlegel and Harris were making so much more money gambling than they might have made with honest jobs, though that certainly was true on good nights. The point was that gambling afforded them an opportunity to make as much money doing what they wanted to as they would have made doing what they had to. Schlegel and Harris watched their parents do what they had to; when they discovered a way to get paid for doing what they wanted to, they discovered the rest of their lives.

Even when they did take on day jobs, as Harris did for a few years when he became an assistant in his father's exterminating business, they still found ways of squeezing more money out of a day's work than most. Shop owners would see Harris walking up the block with the case that identified him as an exterminator—a black case with brass handles and three compartments, one that held his spray gun, another with the concentrated chemical he mixed with water to spray, and another with D.D.T. If any shop owner asked Harris to spray his store on the way to his destination, he always happily obliged for a fee of $5. He only had to spray a minuscule amount of mist to do the job, so his father never noticed and Harris was a little richer for it. One day, Harris's father, who had been saving up his son's income for him because he knew it would be squandered otherwise, told him he had $1,500 saved. Harris quit on the spot and opened a pro shop, where he would drill bowling balls during the day and gamble through the night for the next five years.

As for Schlegel, bowling had always been a way for him to prove he was every bit as wily as any other street kid. The only reason he originally set foot in a bowling alley was to defy high school administrators at Bronx Vocational High School who told him he could not graduate because he did not have a required gym credit. So he joined the bowling team. The swimming team also was an option, but he preferred not to freeze out in the elements of New York's unforgiving fall and winter days. Bowling was an indoor sport that promised to protect him from the elements while also providing that needed gym credit.

Schlegel had gotten his first taste of the sport of bowling as a pinboy up in a small town in New York called Palenville, a hamlet on the outskirts of the Catskills where his parents took him during the summer to keep him out of trouble. Schlegel got his summertime gig as a pinboy at the town's four-lane bowling alley at age 14. He loved the bowling as much as he loved the soda fountain there.

There were many things for kids to love about a Palenville summer in the 1950s: the swimming holes where they could catch fish in the falls that gushed off the mountainsides; the dances at J.C. Johnny's; the gardens pregnant with blackberries, raspberries, huckleberries, and vegetables kids loaded into crates and took back home. Schlegel entered the garden with a cigarette smoking out of each side of his mouth because he believed it kept the mosquitos away. Bugs were a problem; the leaves of potato plants crawled with them, and it took as much work to flick them all away as it took to uproot and bag the produce.

Schlegel's father made sure his son understood that the berries were for his family, not for his mouth.

"One for you and then two for the basket, not two and then one!" he would yell at his son.

Schlegel brought garbage cans loaded with fresh-picked fruit and vegetables back home to New York City. His mother gathered her friends to squash the berries and make jam, which his Aunt Lee used to fill her renowned crepes.

A couple years later Schlegel discovered this bowling thing was something he could do. By the end of his first season bowling for school, he was the team's best player. He began his senior year as captain of the bowling team. By the start of the bowling season in the fall of 1962, he was bowling four leagues a week. He bowled Mondays at Ridgewood Lanes in Brooklyn, Tuesdays at Pinewood Lanes on 125th and Broadway in Manhattan, Wednesdays at Whitestone Lanes in Queens, and Thursdays at Manhattan Lanes just around the corner from the apartment where he lived with his parents at 42 Sickles Street in the Inwood section of Upper Manhattan. He soon heard about something called "pot games," a form of bowling in which all participants tossed a quarter into a pot and bowled a game. The man who bowled the highest score pocketed all the quarters. At a time when people might have brought home between $50-$60 a week in pay, a kid making four or five bucks a day bowling pot games had a viable, full-time job on his hands. Schlegel soon heard about guys in the neighborhood who thought they were better than he was. He went to the places where they bowled and challenged them to head-to-head matches for any amount they cared to wager—action matches, they were called—and he found himself eminently capable of proving them wrong. Those quarters he won bowling pot games soon turned into dollars he won bowling action matches. Then those dollars soon turned into C-notes, and he knew he had found the thing he would do for the rest of his life.

The sport that action bowlers like Schlegel knew was entirely the same sport known to the tens of millions of bowlers who hit the lanes across the United States each year by the early 1960s. Nothing about the game itself was different. The lane was still sixty feet long from foul line to headpin and nearly forty-two inches in width, the bowling ball still twenty-seven inches in circumference and a maximum weight of sixteen pounds, the pins still twelve inches apart and ranging in weight between 3.2 and 3.10 pounds. Like Schlegel, the vast majority of action bowlers—or adult male bowlers generally—threw sixteen-pound bowling balls at the time. Women and children might be more likely to throw lighter bowling balls; the lighter the ball, the less hitting power it had when it collided with the pins. Some tournament directors, such as John Vargo, who ran the famed Vargo Classic in New York City, ensured the pins themselves would be harder to knock down at his tournament by filling them with lead. That brought the weight of the pins closer to four pounds. It also made them bottom-heavy, as he planted lead in them through a hole he drilled in the bottom of each pin. The pins sometimes responded by behaving as though they were anchored to the pin deck. A bowler who won Vargo's tournament knew he had earned it.

The lanes themselves still were made of wood in the early 1960s—maple for the first fifteen feet of the lane followed by forty-five feet of pine, a softer wood, and then maple again for the pin deck, where the pins stood. Maple, a stronger wood, helped the front part of the lane withstand the bruising it sustained as bowlers threw ball after ball. It also helped the pin decks survive the pounding of pins as bowling balls blasted them around.

Scoring, too, was the same for action bowlers as it was for any bowler. A strike still counted for ten points plus the total pin fall accumulated over the next two shots; a spare counted for ten points plus the next shot. A strike on the first shot of the tenth frame allowed a bowler two more shots; a spare allowed one more. A 300 game required twelve consecutive strikes. Bowlers who stepped over the foul line got a score of zero for that shot. Electronic foul lights, invented in the late 1930s, buzzed when a bowler stepped or slid over the foul line and had long-ago eliminated the need for foul line judges by the 1960s. Not every bowling center had installed them, however, and those that did would not always turn them on.

The thing that elevated these ground rules to the realm of "action" was gambling. And the thing that distinguished action bowling from those pot games Schlegel bowled as a kid was the head-to-head match—one guy putting his money down against another's for a game to see who truly was the best. Gamblers behind the lanes—a part of the action bowling scene colloquially referred to as "the back"—placed their bets on the bowler they thought had the best chance of winning. If enough gamblers in the back put money on a particular match, the bowlers themselves could end up bowling for many thousands of dollars in a night.

"Action" itself had nothing to do with bowling; gamblers found action in many forms. Those not bowling a match or betting on one were laying their money down on a game of dice in the parking lot, holding poker hands close to their chests in the lounge, or itching to head out to Yonkers Raceway and bet on the ponies. They made money pitching pencils at parking signs or flipping matchbook covers. Steve Harris and his buddies placed bets on who would have the most attractive woman sit next to them on the subway when they headed back home at dawn. If a large older lady sat next to one of them, they would fall on the floor laughing. Taking the bet was the rush.

Even when gamblers found the action they were looking for in the bowling alley, it was not always as simple as just betting on the guy they thought would win. The bowling alley was not the racetrack. Some matches featured one guy using only two fingers while the other used only his thumb; others featured bowlers who were blindfolded or threw balls between their legs or between chairs arranged on the lane. Action bowlers were gamblers first and bowlers second, and they found the action anywhere they looked for it. The action itself was the objective, regardless of what form it took.

This was the early 1960s, when Atlantic City's rise as a gambling mecca still was years away, no one really spoke of going to Vegas because it felt so distant as to be somewhere on the other side of the world, and even the Meadowlands Racetrack was yet to be built. Off-track betting (OTB) had not yet been legalized. Hustlers may have scratched the gambler's itch in pool halls back in the 1930s and '40s, but by 1962 the bowling alley was the place where they found what they were looking for. And they looked for however long it took to find it.

Schlegel may or may not have known it then, but any time he headed to a bowling alley looking to score some dough, he embraced a heritage that went back hundreds of years. Bowling's dalliance with gambling actually dates back many centuries; bowling did not just become the locus of gamblers and shylocks in Schlegel's New York City youth. In fact, King Henry VIII of England banned bowling in 1511 because of the sport's appeal to society's underbelly. Bowling alleys then were called "alleys" because that is exactly what they were— outdoor alleys usually attached to saloons, taverns, and other places gamblers frequented. As versions of the sport made their way into Germany in the third century and later throughout Europe, bowling continued to be an outdoor activity. America would not see its first indoor bowling alley until 1840, when a place called Knickerbocker Alleys opened in New York City with lanes made of baked clay. King Henry VIII's 1511 ban still was in effect then—it lasted until 1845—even though members of his own court, as well as his successors over the centuries, partook nonetheless. Archaeologists have unearthed evidence of bowling's origins in ancient Egypt, and evidence also suggests that a version of the sport was played in the Stone Age. Given the sport's longstanding affiliation with gambling, it would hardly be surprising if archaeological evidence someday proves that even bowlers in those early societies could not resist the urge to place a bet.

Bowling resumed as a magnet for gamblers in Schlegel's New York City youth because of a boom in bowling center construction hastened by the advent of automatic pinsetters in the early 1950s. Until then, bowling alley proprietors relied on pinboys to keep their doors open. If they had no one to set the pins, they had no customers. Pinboys tended to be sewer-mouthed street urchins proprietors hired while holding their noses, covering their ears, and looking the other way. The bruised, fractured, or bleeding shins pinboys suffered on the job served as evidence of the gruff ilk they represented. World War II ensured that pinboys were in short supply, forcing bowling alleys to reduce their hours of operation or shut down altogether. The American Machine & Foundry Company (AMF) successfully designed and manufactured the first automatic pinsetters, and the Brunswick Corporation later followed suit. The elimination of pinboys completely revolutionized the sport by ushering it into a glittery new era. Women felt welcome in the bowling alley more than ever before now that pinboys were gone and lavish, space-age decor replaced the dingy, claustrophobic, and poorly lit bowling alleys of subway stations and bar basements with spacious, inviting establishments. Bans placed on bowling by local governments in Connecticut and New York—for the same reasons King Henry VIII did so hundreds of years prior—now were lifted, allowing young people to frequent bowling alleys again. Suddenly, the bowling alley was a place to take the family, and soon neighborhoods throughout the United States featured many places to bowl. Most crucially for the action bowling scene, many of these new bowling alleys stayed open around the clock. When the families headed home, the gamblers headed in.

Schlegel enjoyed the fruits of this development himself when Manhattan Lanes, a massive, 62-lane bowling alley, opened on Broadway and Sherman Avenue in Inwood. It was one of the larger bowling alleys in the country at the time. Many other bowling alleys speckled his neighborhood; he hardly could walk a few blocks without passing at least a couple of them. With their abundance and proximity, bowling alleys fulfilled a craving that was not always easily satisfied in an era before Atlantic City casinos or OTB. They ensured that the next bet always was just a block away, if not right across the street. And in the bowling alley, unlike a game of dice or cards, you truly were in charge of your own destiny. You could arrange to bowl a match against a guy you knew had the same average as you; or you could hustle an opponent into underestimating your skill and then bleed the sucker's pockets dry. It also helped that bowling offered a particularly cheap option for gamblers—a game of bowling was just fifty cents in 1962. A pair of rental shoes might set you back twenty cents.

By the time Schlegel discovered Manhattan Lanes around the corner from the Sickles Street apartment he lived in with his parents, bowling was becoming the way for him to live up to something his father told him in 1958, something that would stick with him for the rest of his life.

"The Schlegel name is *our* name! It is your mother's name! And you better not ruin it!" Schlegel's father told him after standing beside his son in court while a judge administered jail terms to his pocketbook-snatching friends. Schlegel had been caught hanging with the wrong crowd in Inwood. One day, he joined a few neighborhood kids as they waited in the subway tunnel at 190th and Broadway. As soon as they spotted an old lady, one of the kids Schlegel was with—a guy named Charlie who was known as "The Beak" thanks to a sizable nose—would do his best to scare the shit out of her. Then two other kids, Wally and his sister Holly, would grab her pocketbook and they all would run.

"What the fuck am I doing here?" Schlegel thought. "What the hell am I doing?"

But there was nowhere left to run the day Charlie scared one old lady well enough to give her a heart attack. They ran all the way to Sherman Avenue and Broadway, down to Jimmy's Candy Store. And that is where they ran into the cops who were looking for them. Charlie got a year-and-a-half. So did Holly. Then the judge turned to Wally. Those sentences might have been a lot longer had the woman not survived.

"You should be ashamed of yourself, teaching your little sister to behave this way!" he said. "I should take you out back right now and whip you myself."

Wally got three years; twice what his sister received. Then, as the judge turned to Schlegel, Schlegel's father had a word for his son.

"No Schlegel has ever gone to jail," he said.

Schlegel's father was a barrel-chested superintendent of the apartment building where they lived, a hard-working man stuffed into a stocky frame of five-foot-six known to treat the local garbage men to a free shot of scotch when the weather got cold. He had a thick, German accent and bulging biceps he liked to flex once in a while just to make sure Schlegel knew he could kick his ass. One day he discovered a particularly subtle way of discouraging drug use in his son's life. He opened a closet that contained a shotgun, pointed at it, and explained the following:

"You see this gun," he said in his gruff, German accent. "It's got a two-round load. One for each eye. I blow your fucking brains out if you ever touch drugs."

That was the father Schlegel feared in court that day, the one who made eminently believable threats involving guns and brawn. He had met with the judge beforehand and persuaded him that he could hand down no justice in court worse than the justice his son would face at home.

"It seems your father will be taking care of this himself," the judge said.

The judge probably had a good ass-kicking in mind, too.

But it was the shame that hurt Schlegel more than any ass-kicking, this negative way of seeing his family's name that meant something more than skin deep. That was the way Schlegel's father had of "taking care" of things—making Schlegel feel ashamed of himself. For Schlegel, no ass-kicking could hurt more than that. From that day on, he had a notion that to bear your family's name is to bear the responsibility of representing it with honor and dignity. That day, perhaps, was the first day he saw himself not just as another kid on the streets, but as a Schlegel. It would be years before Schlegel fully appreciated the extent to which his father spared him that day from the life that might have awaited him had he been hauled off to Juvie.

By then, Schlegel and Harris were on their way out of their parents' apartments and into the lives that awaited them. They both had figured out that they would butter their own bread in life, and that the type of talent Schlegel possessed was not the stuff you put on a resume. No, this was the kind of raw gift that either made you or broke you. This was survival. Now, as life nudged them into their twenties, they had no needling mothers to answer to, no one back home worrying about where they were and asking questions when they finally returned. Here was the freedom they had waited for forever. And tonight, that freedom would be found at a Philadelphia bowling alley just off Route 1.

Hours before Harris hopped into Nagai's Cadillac to head down to Philly, he called up Schlegel and said, "Ernie, we got a fish in Philadelphia!"

A "fish" in action bowling parlance was a sucker whose money was easy because he either didn't know his competition or he had an exaggerated sense of his own abilities. And if he did know his competition and chose therefore to keep his money to himself, well, there were remedies for that: You could ask him to please confirm he still had a pair of balls between his legs, show up on crutches and say you had the gout to put on the airs of easy prey, or start a match with a few thrown games before stunning the poor bastard with enough strikes to make him beg to keep enough money for the bus. You did whatever it took to get him on the lanes and make his money yours. That was the bottom line. Schlegel's bait to catch these fish included the shot of bourbon he downed and the extra splash he rubbed behind his ears, and the long-sleeved shirts he wore to perpetuate rumors that they concealed heroin tracks. And then there was the crooked mouth and the thing his friends called "the twisted eye." Schlegel's vision was so poor in one eye that he tightened it into a kind of contorted squint when he bowled. It made him look a little crazy to the unsuspecting. Despite his impaired vision, Schlegel was the most accurate bowler in New York, an asset that made him not just a good bowler, but a great bowler. He threw a much straighter ball than most; a lot of bowlers at least hooked the ball a little, some a lot. Schlegel preferred a straighter shot because he knew that he never would miss his target, while bowlers with big hooks will not always be able to predict where their ball will end up as it makes its way toward the pins. There is a narrower margin for error when you rely on hook instead of accuracy. When you throw a straighter shot you remove that uncertainty; and when you know, too, that you rarely will miss the target you are looking at, you are a fearsome competitor.

But for Schlegel, action bowling was as much about hustling as it was about physical ability—the way a stench of bourbon or a twist in the eye consumed more of his opponent's focus than the match itself. And that was exactly the point: You wanted the guy on the other side of the ball return to think about anything but how to get out of the place with money in his pocket, anything but what he had done to succeed in this spot before. You had to convince the fish that there was something wrong with you, afflict him with the delusion that he had the upper hand. If you played your part well, your prey would get angry—so angry, in fact, that he would bet far more money than reason advised. The double-or-nothings, the big bills he would lay down to recoup those small bills his buddies had just watched him lose, the machismo that gnawed at him as his humiliation grew. That's when you made the real money; that's when you were playing a game Schlegel liked to call "the spider and the fly." By the time Schlegel's opponents found themselves down a couple hundred bucks, they knew they were caught.

The roommates Schlegel would soon live with knew he played the role of the spider well enough to send him bowling whenever they needed some rent money. They knew about the night Schlegel and his chain-smoking doubles partner, Johnny Campbell, took on the most fearsome duo in action bowling, a pair of bowlers known as Fats and Deacon, in a 12-hour match that culminated in a tie at dawn. Both teams piled their cash on the score table for one last game to settle it all. With fingers so raw by then that the finger holes in their bowling balls were stained with blood, they once again battled down to the 10th frame, when Schlegel needed all three strikes to win the match. He stepped up and threw what Campbell would describe for years to come as the best three strikes he ever saw in his life. The money was theirs.

But Schlegel and his act found fewer takers by 1962. After a while, even the fish came to know your shtick well enough to call it bullshit. It was time to take that act on the road, away from New York City. Philly seemed as promising a stage as any.

No matter where the scent of fish happened to lead, Schlegel followed it the way a coyote follows the trail of a dying animal. From Queens to Connecticut, from Paramus to Pennsylvania, no destination was too far off if it promised to bring in the cash. Toru Nagai and his Cadillac made sure of that. In his mid-thirties, Toru was older than Schlegel and the boys by nearly twenty years. To a cadre of degenerate gamblers too young to drive but desperate to follow the scent of money wherever it took them, a guy with a car was a precious commodity. And to hunt for fish in a Cadillac, no less? That was a teen gambler's dream.

Back then, the closest Schlegel and Harris came to having a car of their own was by stealing one. Harris's brother had a car, and some nights Harris waited around for him to fall asleep so he could steal his car keys. The only stop he made on his way to the nearest action was to pick up his walking jackpot—Ernie Schlegel. Then the night, and the money it promised, was theirs. All Harris had to do was make it back home by the time his brother had to get up for work, and pray no one had taken his parking spot in the meantime. Somehow, no one ever did.

On this particular night, Schlegel found his fish in the form of a hotshot down in Philly who said he would bowl anybody who dared to show up at his home alley. Harris did the man the favor of informing him that a fellow by the name of Ernie Schlegel would be quite happy to oblige his offer, but that before agreeing to bowl him he might want to consider the very real possibility that Schlegel would hand him his ass and charge him for it. Harris could talk that way by then. He had just watched the guy challenge his buddy Richie Solomon to $25 a game and bowl him to an even draw after several hours. A bowler of Schlegel's caliber this was not. If the man could not get the best of Richie Solomon after three hours of trying his damnedest to do so, then he sure as shit would not get the best of Ernie Schlegel.

"You've got to be kidding me! You're not that good," Harris told him.

"I am telling you, I will bowl anybody," he said.

"Well, Ernie's really good. I mean, he's much better than you," Harris warned.

"I will bowl him," he said.

Harris told him Schlegel would be quite happy to drop by the following weekend and see if the guy was as good as he thought he was. And come the following weekend they did, pulling up to the joint in style with Nagai's obsidian Caddy.

No one could have blamed the fish if he thought he had found a fish of his own the first time he laid eyes on Schlegel. With a head of long, strawberry-blond hair so unkempt it might have looked like home to passing crows, a wrinkled set of clothes that gave off a vague whiff of having been worn at least for the past several days, and a face he hadn't shaved in weeks, Schlegel did not exactly cut the figure of a kid in possession of any particular skill, much less a prodigy. And thanks to an infection in his gums caused by a dentist's botched attempt to fill some cavities as a child, he also had lost most of his teeth. Action bowling winnings soon would help him replace them, but for now their absence helped harden his disarming facade.

In short, Schlegel looked more like a hobo who lived in an abandoned taxi than like a hustler. And that, of course, was how the hustle worked. That was the bait. Gone were the days of pool hall hustlers in three-piece suits who powdered their hands between matches. Here was a hustler who looked like the kid that emptied Fast Eddie Felson's ashtray, who was remarkable only for the extent to which he looked so unremarkable. The only physical attribute that betrayed the brazenness within were his eyes. Schlegel's eyes seemed to have a kind of cast about them, a mean pair of reptilian squints that looked like two crude gashes in a jack-o-lantern. Paired with a nose vaguely gnarled by the blows that broke it in street brawls and dragnets, and those paying attention might have known better than to put their money at risk.

Most who hadn't heard Schlegel's name or just did not know any better—and there were enough of those types to keep the money coming in, especially outside New York—happily agreed to take him on. They sized him up as an easy target. There always was a fish who took him for just another drunk or druggie with nothing better to do with his money than lose it. They smelled the bourbon and saw the rags that passed for clothing; they did not look hard enough to find the man behind them. It never took long before Schlegel opened up his back pocket and let them fill it. If the fish didn't have a dollar, Schlegel would find one.

Schlegel found more than a dollar down in Philly the night he went fishing there with Nagai and Harris, thrashing the man who said he'd bowl anybody and banking a quick $200. And that, in hindsight, is where his Philly exploits ought to have ended. But when that bottom line is yielding just enough cash to pique your hunger for more, it's awfully easy to talk about what should have been. Here in Philly, in 1962, the money flowed like beer from a tap, and home was more than two hours up the road. You don't just drive from New York to Philly to bowl four games and leave, even if staying meant risking it all.

Harris would soon have every reason to worry, but for now the vanquished local stunned Schlegel and the boys with a flourish of class they rarely encountered in smoke-filled bowling alleys after dark.

"It was a pleasure bowling you guys," he said. "If you want to really make some money, there's a bowling alley out on

Route 1 in New Jersey called Federal Lanes. And the manager there will bowl anybody for any amount. He's like a *superstar* in that bowling alley, but you're better than him and you can take him. So why don't you go there?"

Call it the voice of greed. Call it the voice of the devil himself. But whatever force compelled that Philadelphia fish to lure them down Route 1, Schlegel and the boys heard it loud and clear. Down Route 1 they went in the pitch darkness of night. They would find the fish they went looking for at Federal Lanes, but they also would find the kind of people who only come out at night, the ones who will just as soon plant a blade in your eye as they will shake your hand.

It was one in the morning by the time the Caddy pulled up to Federal Lanes. They found the manager closing up shop for the night. But they didn't come to help the guy mop his floors and turn out the lights; they came to relieve him of his cash. They asked him if he wanted to bowl, told him they heard he liked action.

"Sure," he said.

Then they started bowling. That, as Schlegel and the boys were about to learn, was their first mistake.

Once again, Nagai's prized pony performed well enough to recoup every dime of gas money he spent to take him there and much more, besting the "superstar" for hours on end until the first glow of dawn blanched the bowling alley windows. This guy was no pretender like the one who couldn't even take down Richie Solomon back at Jimmy Dykes's place back in Philly. This was a real bowler, a good bowler. Still, Schlegel was better. By five in the morning, the manager called it quits.

Then the chumps walked in.

They were a gang of kids in their mid-to late teens looking to keep the match going by putting their money on the manager.

Harris knew a fish when he smelled one, and these kids reeked of it. But he also knew exhaustion when he felt it. By the time the kids arrived, Harris had fallen half asleep in the settee area behind another pair of lanes, spent by the long day of traveling far and wide to find places where the fish dwelled. Schlegel decided he would indeed resume the match. Harris told this new school of fish he would cover whatever bets they had.

The kids started putting up seven bucks here, three bucks there. They were the kinds of small bets Schlegel wasn't used to back home, but there were at least eight of these kids, and between them all plus what the manager was betting it was an okay bet.

After twenty-four hours of shutting the biggest mouths in bowling alleys from Philly to South Jersey without so much as a minute's sleep in the meantime, all it took was "an okay bet" to rouse Steve Harris from his half-conscious slumber. That's all it ever took when you were in on the action. After all, it was gambling that sent Schlegel and the boys down Route 1 to Jimmy Dykes Lanes, gambling that sent them deep into south Jersey on the trail of the fish they smelled there, gambling that roused Harris from his sleep the moment a pack of hoods with change to spare emerged from the night. Schlegel laced up his shoes again, Harris tallied all the money the kids dared to spare on a man who had no answer for Ernie Schlegel, the machine set yet another rack of pins, and the games, once again, began. By now the "superstar" that Harris and Schlegel heard about back in Philly looked like little more than a super sucker. His next few games did nothing to demonstrate otherwise. Schlegel beat him again. The guy called it quits, and the night, finally, was over.

Or so Harris thought.

Some of the bowlers Harris knew back home might take a bad night of losses in stride and try their luck again the following night, but the boys Harris did business with down in Jersey were the kind that did not wait until next time to get their money back. No, these were the kinds of gamblers who only lost when they agreed to, who only went home with empty pockets if the other guys brought bigger knives than they did.

Schlegel packed his ball and shoes again. Harris slipped back into the half-sleep he'd fallen into before these kids came around looking to score. And that is when the night they never would forget began. Harris heard the sound of kids slamming bowling balls into the floor and damning to hell the "New York hustlers" Nagai had brought to town. Only feigning sleep now, Harris listened as the kids openly discussed the speed and trajectory at which a bowling ball must be thrown to blow open a grown man's head like a butternut squash at a shooting range. That, of course, was the end of even the pretense of sleep. That, perhaps, was the moment Harris found himself more fully awake than ever before. A realization that the next time you do catch some sleep may in fact be the last time will tend to do that to you.

Harris stood up.

"What's your problem?" he asked the kids. "We're not hustlers. We didn't come in here pretending we didn't know how to bowl, asking if you will teach us how to bowl like they do in a pool hall. We came in and Ernie said 'Do you want to bowl?' That means he's good! We know the manager's good, and Ernie's good. That's not hustling. Ernie beat him fair and square!'"

Mere reason may have been enough to get them out of jams back in New York City, but down in south Jersey, reason was no match for a knife. The shortest kid among them busted out a blade. Switchblade knives were popular in those days, but this was something closer to a box cutter. When the kid pushed a button, the blade came straight out, and it was half-an-inch wide like a razor blade. He pressed the blade against Harris's belly and explained exactly what he intended to do with it.

"You're gonna die, motherfucker," the kid told him.

Harris shut his mouth; this was new territory for him. Schlegel and Nagai were gathering their belongings several lanes away with their backs turned, oblivious.

———•———

Despite the abundance of cash gamblers tossed around in the biggest action houses, muggings were still virtually unheard of. Maybe one heard about matches that began with bowling balls and ended with guns, but you never saw it happen yourself. You knew where the dangerous bowling alleys were and you stayed away. Nonetheless, if you were an action player in New York City, you knew the stories.

You knew about the night Kenny Barber, one of the greatest action bowlers of all time, found himself caught in a tough match against a local legend named Mike Chiu-chiolo. How Barber had to walk up to the mobsters who put their money on him and tell them he thought maybe he just didn't have it that night. The fear he felt when they told him they "weren't losing tonight," his realization that they were packing enough guns to hold the place up if Barber lost their money. You knew the relief that came to a seventeen-year-old kid who was only looking to leave the place with some extra money and instead thanked his lucky stars to be leaving with his life.

And then there was the night Jim Byrnes headed down to Green Acres, Long Island, with some buddies to bowl a night of action.

Byrnes showed up with his friend Billy Spigner and a kid named Brian Hayes, an up-and-coming action player whose talent was as formidable as his addiction to blow. Some kids bowled during the day so they had money to throw down at the racetrack at night; others bowled because it was the only thing that made them feel alive. Hayes bowled so he could make the money he needed to buy his next fix.

After a few back-and-forth matches that did not yield much in return, Hayes suggested they bowl for $700 a game. In the early 1960s, that was as much as some people earned in three months at their day jobs. Byrnes said, "Okay." A couple frames into the next game, Byrnes realized that might prove to be one of the last things he would ever say.

In the second frame, Spigner walked over to Byrnes, who was sitting at the score table. He leaned in and whispered, "If you lose the match, run to the lot! We don't have enough money to pay them."

Byrnes knew the gangsters betting in the back did not take kindly to kids who had the balls to bet with money they did not have. He knew these were the kinds of guys who sent bodyguards to toss debtors through plate glass windows, humorless troglodytes with fingers thick as cannolis. And he knew there were dozens of them putting their money down on his opponent, a guy named Tommy Delutz Sr. If Byrnes lost the game, the possibility that he also might lose his life was significant enough that his bowling ball felt like somebody had glued it to his hand when he tried to let go of it—a problem known in bowling as "squeezing" the ball. The more you let your nerves dominate you on the lanes, the tighter you grip your bowling ball and it feels as though the ball will not come off of your thumb at the release. More often than not, the squeezers turn out to be the losers.

Byrnes needed all three strikes in the 10th frame to win the game, or the first two strikes and then nine pins to tie.

The way the ball was coming off his hand, his best shot was to fire it directly at the pocket as hard as he possibly could. On the first shot, it worked. The ball took two revs down the lane and landed in the pocket for a strike. Then it worked again.

"Please, God, give me nine!" Byrnes thought to himself. "Let us tie so I can get the fuck out of here!"

Then he threw another strike.

"Those were the greatest shots you ever threw!" Spigner told him.

"Yeah, seven hundred dollars and our lives? That ain't bad!" Byrnes said.

Then he threw up.

But it was not good enough for Hayes, who suggested they bowl again.

"Brian," Byrnes said, "let me swallow my stomach first!"

But they did bowl again, and they went home a couple grand richer by the time the night was through. But it was clear to them that the world of action bowling was moving in a deadlier direction.

———•———

Steve Harris knew the stories as well as anyone. As he stood in Federal Lanes with a blade pressed against him, he knew this was not the first time an action bowler had ended up on the wrong end of a gangster's knife, and he knew it would not be the last.

Before the kid made good on his promise to send Harris on a one-way trip out of this world, he had a question for him.

"Are you a Jew?" the kid said.

This was a question Harris had heard too many times before. He thought of the winter mornings he descended into the subway station tunnel on his walk to school to avoid the cold in his native Inwood, then a predominantly Irish neighborhood, and the Irish Catholic kids who would wait on the other side to beat him because their parents told them the Jews killed Jesus. He remembered how petrified he was to walk those streets with the velvet bag that contained his tallit, the Jewish prayer shawl he received on his bar mitzvah which he took with him to the temple up the block on the High Holy Days. How he would hold it close to his body so the neighborhood bullies would not see the Star of David embroidered on it.

Jewish kids growing up in the Inwood of Harris's youth knew they were in for a beating if they dared enter any of the neighborhood's seventy-three Irish pubs. Good Shepherd Church near the bustling intersection of 207th Street and Broadway hosted no less than fourteen masses packed with Irish Catholics every Sunday, and a xenophobic paranoia thickened the air with rumors about the "negroes" moving in and the jobs and homes they would steal from Irish families who had lived there for generations. The black, Puerto Rican, and Jewish children of Inwood grew up with a nagging feeling they were some foreign presence discourteously taking up residence on somebody else's turf. To be different from the rest on those streets, and especially to have had the audacity to be born a Jew, was to live your life as a marked man. And now, a couple of hours down the road from all that, here was a south Jersey hood with his knife pressed to Harris's gut and a question all too familiar to a kid from those angry streets back home. Maybe, for the first time in his life, he found himself yearning for those days when the worst thing he had to worry about was what to say to his mother when he made it back home just before dawn. Maybe that freedom he went chasing when he left her house for good also was something to fear.

Persuading the kid he had not been hustled had been worth a shot, but there was not much Harris could do about his Jewishness. His first instinct was to tell the kid that no, he was not a Jew. But then he figured that if being Jewish was the thing he was about to die for, he would rather die proudly than die a coward.

"Yes, I am," Harris told the kid. "What about it?"

For a moment, everyone was silent.

"No shit?" the kid said. "Me, too! Gimme five!"

The hood put away the blade and stuck out his hand. Harris could not believe it. He hesitated a moment and slapped him five. Then he noticed the kid's expression change.

"What's wrong?"

The kid mewled pathetically about not having any money for breakfast.

If enough dough to buy breakfast was all it would take to spare Harris his life, then breakfast was precisely what these boys would get. Harris learned enough on the streets of New York City to know a can't-miss deal when he saw one. He promptly curled off thirty bucks from his roll of the night's winnings—easily enough in those days to buy breakfast every day for the next week. And, just as quickly, he and Schlegel followed Nagai out of the place, making sure to offer a few kind goodbyes for good measure.

Nagai's Cadillac may have been the reason Schlegel and the boys headed south on Route 1 that night, but there was another reason they liked having the old man along when they went fishing: They knew they could count on him to deliver an ass-kicking as much as they could count on him for a ride. Nagai may have been older and smaller, but he was a guy you did not mess with. Nagai and his cohorts were at least as tough as any of the gangsters they encountered in bowling alleys. One of Nagai's buddies, who stood barely five feet tall and weighed about 150 pounds, once was held up by a few muggers who were twice his size. He told them he had $8, and that he would give each of them $2 and keep the last $2 for bus money to get home. The muggers did not particularly care for diplomacy, however, and demanded all the dough. Seconds later, the biggest of the three was out cold on the ground and the other two were running as fast as they could. Nagai was like that, too, having trained in martial arts himself.

Just as Harris and Schlegel made it to Nagai's car in the parking lot, they found themselves confronted by the whole gang they thought they had bought off inside—only now they were armed to the teeth with chains, knives, pipes and various other implements of persuasion. In the few minutes it took to reach the car, it dawned on the gang that if a knife flash got them $30, a real fight would get them even more. Fortunately the only weapons Nagai usually needed were his own bare hands, and he managed to nearly single-handedly take on the entire gang, with Harris and Schlegel heading for Nagai's Cadillac.

"When you lose, that should be a lesson to you," Nagai admonished with a scowl as he performed a brutal karate chop on the fender of another parked car.

Then Nagai told Schlegel and the boys it was time to get the hell out of there. He knew as well as they did that scaring the hoods was a great way of attracting more of them. Nagai twisted the keys in the ignition of his Caddy and, as he peeled off into the street, lifted a long iron bar from under his seat and twirled it around in his hand. From their vantage point, the gangsters must have sworn he was wielding a gun. If the objective was not to scare the poor bastards, then at that point they could consider the night a total failure, because fear attracted more teens looking for a fight like moths to a porch light. Nagai screamed up Route 1 at about 80 miles an hour with a car full of 'hoods on his tail. They pursued the Caddy for nearly forty miles and, only then, finally conceded that the money they put on the wrong man that night was money they never would see again. Neither Harris nor Schlegel ever considered taking weapons of their own into bowling alleys after that, because the incident was such an aberration in their experience.

It was also the last Nagai and the boys would ever see of Federal Lanes. It was not, however, the last time a coterie of young gamblers went out looking for action and instead found themselves on the wrong end of a gangster's weapon. As 1962 drew to a close, one bowling alley in Brooklyn, New York was emerging as a place where the trouble was at least as plentiful as the treasure. Those who walked the precarious line between the two had stories to tell for the rest of their lives.

2

THE GUNS OF AVENUE M

By 1963, the Brooklyn action bowling scene swirled with rumors about gangsters who packed heat, shylocks who had ways of making sure you did not forget the debt you owed, and con artists who swindled the wrong crowd. Rumor and reality rarely make good bedfellows, of course; most action bowlers who went fishing in Brooklyn made it back home no worse for wear. Others, however, headed home with tales to tell and never dared set foot in the Brooklyn action again. But the promise of a big score overruled any fear the gamblers felt as they headed to Brooklyn for a night of action. Most of the time, they found that action at a place called Avenue M Bowl.

An imposing but otherwise unremarkable edifice, Avenue M Bowl was a two-story bowling alley with lockers and a lounge upstairs. The building stretched from McDonald Avenue to East 2nd Street on Avenue M in Brooklyn, just beside the elevated subway. The owner, Howie Noble, had a face so gnarled with pockmarks that most knew him by his nickname, "Fish Face," an appropriate moniker given his famous tuna sandwiches served at the lunch counter. Served on thick slices of New York deli rye with chips and a Coke for $0.50, the tuna salad contributed to Fish Face's reputation as one of the cheapest guys in town. Patrons suspected that the tuna, tasty as it was, consisted largely of a lower-grade fish called bonito.

The building itself served as the most vivid illustration of Fish Face's frugality. The joyless monotony of its brick exterior, void of even the slightest decorative flourish, amplified the endlessness of its expanse from McDonald Avenue to East 2nd. There was not much more to see inside, where a yawning stretch of blank, white walls deadened the decor. Many bowling alleys display trophy cases, wall murals, plaques, or scoreboards honoring the highest scores ever bowled there. The interior of Avenue M Bowl, however, betrayed a ruthless opposition to such indulgences. Indulgences, after all, cost money, and Fish Face preferred to keep his money where he liked it best—in his pocket. But if the ambiance lacked distinction, the clientele most definitely did not. Avenue M Bowl housed one of the most eclectic collections of characters the action bowling scene ever assembled under one roof, and it was the locus of some of the most unforgettable drama in action bowling history.

Fish Face may have been cheap, but the man knew how to make a buck. Avenue M Bowl, like many New York City bowling alleys at the time, was open 24 hours a day, seven days a week. Fish Face always made a killing on Sunday afternoons, when it seemed as if every family within five miles took their kids out for a few games, and bowling leagues packed the alley most evenings. Late at night, when league bowlers headed home and families had long ago put their kids to bed, the place struggled to rent out a lane or two at a time. Fish Face was not the only proprietor struggling to rent out lanes at the time. Like any bubble bound to burst, proprietors were finding by 1963 that the abundance of bowling alleys built after the automatic pinsetter changed the business forever made it difficult to corner the market of bowlers in a given neighborhood. Bowlers were spreading their patronage across a variety of bowling alleys, all of them close to their homes. Business suffered; bowling alleys began to close down. The Brunswick Corporation repossessed nearly 20,000 pinsetters and more than 15,000 lanes between 1962 and 1966. This misfortune soon proved to be action bowling's gain.

Bubbles may be bound to burst, but good businessmen are bound to hatch good ideas. And Fish Face had an idea. He spotted talent in a couple regulars, a pair of bowlers known as Mac and Stoop who were as renowned for whoring as they were for bowling. When Mac and Stoop were not out on the prowl for women, they were bowling for the money they needed to do so. Fish Face decided to bill them as the most invincible doubles team New York City had ever seen, daring other local players to challenge them to doubles matches for any amount of money they cared to wager. Mac and Stoop happily obliged, taking on challengers after the last leagues concluded, at about midnight or one in the morning. Soon, word on the street had it that there was this place in Brooklyn where a couple of wise guys thought no one could beat them. That was a surefire way to attract many more wise guys, Fish Face soon discovered. And each of them, of course, ranked his ability at least as highly as Mac and Stoop ranked theirs.

Some of the guys who showed up to challenge them matched Fish Face's nickname with monikers of their own, names like

Bernie Bananas or Freddy the Ox, who owed his nickname to the 6'4" frame into which he stuffed his prodigious girth; or Joe The Kangaroo, who took a three-step approach and then hopped around the approach on one leg after each shot.

One night an action bowler from Brooklyn named Johnny Petraglia was watching Joe the Kangaroo bowl a guy called Frankie the Leaper. They both averaged around 130. Johnny watched them throw some practice shots before the match, Joe hopping around in circles and Frankie falling into a push-up position after each shot and leaping back up to his feet. That was just how Joe and Frankie went about things on the lanes. Nobody asked why; they just gave it a name. There was no eccentricity a good name couldn't manage.

Then Johnny heard some gambler say, "I think I'll bet on the Kangaroo tonight. He looks lined up."

The gambler was dead serious. Johnny laughed hard enough to keep laughing for about a week.

But sometimes the real names were just as inimitable, names that evoked visions of murderers convening in alley-ways to determine whose bed would receive the next severed horse head: Sis Montovani, Doc Iandoli, Nunzio Morra, Tony Riccobono. Two of the era's greatest characters comprised a fearsome doubles team known as Fats and Deacon. They were Fats Carozza and Deacon Deconza, the ones who bowled Ernie Schlegel and Johnny Campbell to a bloody draw in a match that began at dusk and ended at dawn. Those were the days before Schlegel had to look for action outside New York because he ran out of willing challengers back home. Schlegel encountered many other characters then, but none of them blasted the pins more emphatically than the Ox, and Fish Face wanted to capitalize on that.

Fish Face only meant to drum up a little more late-night business. He would soon go down as one of the pioneers of action bowling. By 1963, Avenue M Bowl was attracting the greatest action bowlers from New York City and beyond. They came from all five boroughs. They came from Connecticut. They came from Long Island. They came from New Jersey. They came from Chicago, Philadelphia, Boston. They came from everywhere. From custodians to criminals, bankers to bakers, superintendents to salesmen, they came from every station in life in pursuit of the same thing: the rush of adrenaline that promised to come with the next big bet. Gambling, it seemed, was the one unifying passion that dissolved any differences of status or class that resumed the moment they walked out the doors at dawn.

Legions of shouting gamblers waved fistfuls of money at scorekeepers and matchmakers from coast to coast, betting on anything that was betable. Kids flipped coins for money at the lunch counter. Gamblers crowded the locker room with games of craps and cards, following fights and races. And cigar smoke and salty banter thickened the air in the lounge upstairs, where gangsters and shylocks engaged in a number of illicit activities. Those activities included, in no particular order: drinking, cavorting with the revolving door of beautiful women attracted to all that power and money, negotiating loans with dead-broke gamblers who swore they had a fish in their sights, or plotting the demise of other dead-broke gamblers whose debts had grown to such a size that they soon may be just plain dead.

Taking loans you could not repay from the kind of people who made you regret it was only one way gambling could kill you. Sometimes the debauchery at Avenue M Bowl made its way across the street to Danny's Luncheonette, where one day a married salesman who frequented the bowling alley on his off time bet another guy named Paul that he could drink a fifth of scotch straight down. Paul told him he was nuts, so the salesman walked Paul to a nearby liquor store and showed him how real men drank. He drank a fifth of scotch straight down for $50, a lot of money back then. It was the final demonstration of machismo he ever performed. Walking toward East 2nd Street on his way home, he promptly dropped dead in the street.

But risking your life to make good on a bet was no unusual thing. One day somebody bet a gambler named John McNichols that he could not swim across the Hudson River. McNichols swam it one way. Then the guy bet him he could not swim back, and McNichols, unable to resist, took him up on that bet too. He never made it.

If the gambling did not kill you, sometimes it made you wish it had. Al Rosa was a married twenty-something guy who made more money than he needed by working as a fur cutter. When he moved with his wife to an apartment across the street from Avenue M Bowl, he found just the place for people who made more money than they needed and had an itch to spend it. He also found a place where the vultures of action bowling laid in wait for the uninitiated, and Rosa definitely was among the uninitiated. One such vulture was Bernie Bananas, a fifteen-year-old Jewish kid with glasses and good grades who spent his time away from the lanes with his face in a book. Once Bernie found Avenue M Bowl, though, he was spending a lot more time rolling on the lanes than he was spending with his books. No book or classroom possibly could have furnished Bernie with the street wisdom he gleaned at Avenue M—wisdom he used to victimize Rosa.

Rosa got a taste of action at Avenue M Bowl that kept him coming back every payday. Bernie was as adept at spotting fish as any other action bowler, and was reeling Rosa in. He would clean Rosa out of his paycheck every time. Then he would bowl Rosa yet another match on credit so Rosa would have to pay up the next time he got his paycheck. Whenever Rosa walked into Avenue M Bowl it was like a drunk walking in to tend bar. He had to bowl Bernie again, despite the abundant evidence that he had no chance. Word on the street was that Rosa's taste for the action cost him his job and, ultimately, his wife. Some might say Bernie ruined him; others might say Rosa ruined himself. Regardless of how Rosa's paycheck fell into Bernie's hands or what it cost him in things far more lasting than money, the teenaged Bernie was happy to count his cash and keep it coming. Bernie was a thin rung shy of the upper-echelon of great bowlers. Only a handful of bowlers attained those heights, but Bernie still averaged around 195. His peers knew him for a strange approach in which he looked like some bird descending out of the sky to land on the foul line as he made his shot. But Bernie did not need to be great, even though he was close to it. He just needed to know when he was facing inferior talent—better yet, inferior talent with a loose wallet. That helped Bernie accomplish two things: He did not have to bowl exceptionally well to win; and by not bowling exceptionally well, he preserved the image of a guy who could be beaten. A guy like that could always find willing challengers. With all the bowling practice Rosa had given Bernie by then, his game was more refined than ever, further lessening what slight chance of winning Rosa had.

To another enterprising teenager living on 57th Street and 20th Avenue in the Bensonhurst section of Brooklyn, sneaking out to Avenue M Bowl despite a strict father's curfew seemed like a perfectly good reason to risk his life. Fifteen-year-old Clifford Nordquist woke up at three A.M. in an anxious sweat, dreaming of the legends he heard about all day at Avenue M Bowl but had never seen for himself. By then, Nordquist was spending so much time at Avenue M Bowl that the place had become his second home. The old timers who kept their eyes on the kid meant only to entertain him with their stories of what they had seen the night before. But to Nordquist, those stories felt more like torture. His father's ten P.M. curfew fell far too early for him to glimpse the gamblers, gangsters, and shy-locks who filled Fish Face's coffers while the rest of Brooklyn slept. Finally, Nordquist had had enough. He stuffed his blanket with pillows in the hope that it might be enough to allay his father's suspicions. Just in case, he also left a bullshit note about leaving early to go fishing with buddies. Then he opened the window of his second-floor bedroom, lunged from the sill to the peach tree in the yard, climbed down the tree, and walked the half-mile to Avenue M Bowl in the middle of the night.

The sight he beheld as he neared the corner of Avenue M and McDonald was one he would never forget: Rows of pricey cars, double- and triple-parked, circled the block that by day had tractor trucks and beat-up clunkers at the curb. Flood lights over the front entrance cast a glowing spotlight on a gaggle of gamblers loitering outside, the deafening rattle of the elevated subway strung along McDonald Avenue intruding on their conversation. As Nordquist made his way inside, he found every one of the alley's twenty-eight lanes teeming with action—bowlers and gamblers shouting bets and challenges from one end of the place to the other. The place was so thick with people he could hardly make his way through the crowd. It was official: Fish Face had turned those sleepy late nights at Avenue M Bowl into a midnight carnival that seemed to attract every degenerate within a thousand-mile radius.

No one who frequented Avenue M Bowl rivaled the degen-eracy of a hustler known as Iggy Russo. Most action bowlers were kids in their late teens or early 20s, but Russo was dif-ferent. He was older, a guy in his middle forties with a wife, kids and a day job. Given Russo's many rumored transgressions against men who made a hobby of lodging bullets in the temples of those who crossed them, everyone expected Iggy to be found in the Hudson River someday with a boulder tethered to his ankle and a skull freckled with bullet holes. And there was something else everybody knew about Russo: The man never knew a day in his life when he felt the slightest bit of shame—a flaw in his character to which he owed his improbable survival.

Russo contrived the appearance of a no-talent noodle begging to be fleeced of his lunch money. He dressed like a clown, rolling the legs of his pants up to his knees to expose a pair of plaid socks. He wore his black hair closely cropped, and sported a thick pair of glasses and occasionally a duckbill cap. He spoke in a squeaky falsetto many would remember as his most bizarre idiosyncrasy. His reputation as a shyster was so renowned that some suspected the falsetto, too, was part of his act. The standard bowling ball most men used weighed sixteen pounds, as lighter balls were considered to be inferior because they provided less hitting power than a ball of maximum weight. But Russo drove up with a trunk full of balls and pins loaded with lead that made them harder to knock down, just as John Vargo did with the pins in his tournament to make conditions more challenging. If you wanted to bowl Russo for any amount of money, you accepted his props as part of the deal. You played by Russo's rules.

Russo was not fooling those in the know, however. The good bowlers knew Russo had far more talent than he let on. On a Friday night in 1958, Russo showed up at another Brooklyn bowling alley called Park Circle Lanes, got on the microphone, and challenged anyone in the place to a match. Any bowler with common sense knew that somebody who had the balls to walk into a Brooklyn bowling alley and take on the house had some serious game; no one took him up on his offer. Russo, as always, was there to make money, not to cater to a house full of cowards. So, lacking any takers for a head to head match, he found someone who would take the bet of $100 that he could bowl 120 on the nose. Russo promptly strung together five consecutive strikes in the first five frames—which added up to a total score of 120. A strike is ten points plus the next two balls. So a game that begins with five strikes followed by nothing but gutter balls, which are worth zero points, adds up to thirty points in the first frame, sixty in the second, ninety in the third, one-hundred-and-ten in the fourth and one-hundred-and-twenty in the fifth. No one needed to explain the math to Russo. If the man knew anything, he knew how to keep score in a game of bowling. The other thing he knew was that he could walk into a bowling alley and string together five strikes at will. But that was a flourish of ability he preferred to exhibit only before an audience of disbelievers who paid in cash. He swiped his C-note from the score table and asked his victim if he cared to do any further business.

By the time Russo made Avenue M Bowl the locus of his machinations, he learned that there was a lot more money in hustling than there was in stunning the unsuspecting with his skill. Why bother showing them how good you were if no one dared to bowl you? Russo needed to feign vulnerability; he needed to play that game Ernie Schlegel called "the spider and the fly." Russo would prove to be one of the city's most able spiders. He became a "dumper"—the epithet reserved for bowlers who secretly bet against themselves and then bowled badly on purpose to score some easy dough. Russo hardly was the only dumper in the action bowling scene; he just happened to be the most brazen and notorious of them all. The specter of dumpers soon would imperil action bowling as it was known, as bowlers tired of trying to discern between gamblers and crooks. If your opponent missed a spare, you wanted to believe he missed it because he threw an errant shot, not because he secretly was scheming to bowl badly on purpose for his own personal gain. You wanted to believe that the difference between an action match and a boxing match in the 1960s was that the action match was not fixed. As dumpers eroded that notion, they eroded an era. Even Ernie Schlegel regarded Russo as a bad apple that threatened to ruin the batch, the kind of con man who might have driven away many fish who thought, thanks to Russo's shenanigans, that the whole action bowling scene was rigged. But on one night in particular—the night witnesses would tell about for the rest of their lives—Russo, for once, proved too smart for his own good.

Russo was locked in a match against a bowler named Pat Feely, who also was known to dump matches. Russo, as usual, had bet against himself and was bowling as badly as he possibly could. He had to bowl particularly poorly on this occasion, though, because Feely, unbeknownst to Russo, happened to be betting against himself as well. By the 10th frame, Russo was leading by a score of 156-155, which was exceptionally low for bowlers of their well-known talent level. Russo and Feely each had their backer, guys who funded the match with their own stolen cash. Most backers fit the same profile: tobacco-stained fingers the size of meat hooks; huge, gnarled noses that looked like tubas; massive, balding heads of silver hair, and suits tailored so expertly they looked like a layer of skin. Their expressions remained as unsmiling in times of fortune as they did in times when they had to rain unspeakable harm on enemies and debtors. Most people thought they were in the mob. But if they ever considered making that suspicion known to others, they usually thought better about it. Backers prowled the action bowling scene for good bowlers to bet on and, if they were as good as they thought they were, ride them to riches. With each backer betting on the other guy to win the match between Russo and Feely, and with the scores as miserable as they were, the backers started to suspect foul play.

The problem for Russo and Feely was that most backers—especially those at Avenue M Bowl—were the kind who brought guns to the party.

Russo got up in the 10th frame and left the 2-4-5 on his first shot. That spare combination, a cluster of pins in the left half of the rack, is one of the most common leaves for a right-handed player, and it often is the result of what bowlers call a "light" hit. The ten pins in bowling are arranged in four rows, with the headpin having the first row to itself. The headpin, or 1 pin, is followed by a row of two pins, the 2 and 3. That is followed by a row of three pins, the 4, 5 and 6, which is followed by the final row of pins in the back of the rack, the 7, 8, 9 and 10. The addition of one pin per row allows the rack of pins to be arranged in its triangular shape. When a right-handed player properly strikes the area between the 1 and 3 pins known as the "pocket," the ball itself actually only collides with four of the ten pins in the rack—the 1 pin, the 3 pin, the 5 pin, and the 9 pin. Each of those collisions sets the rest of the strike in motion. The 1 pin takes out the 2, 4, and 7 pins; the 3 pin takes out the 6 and 10 pins; the 5 pin takes out the 8 pin and the ball itself takes care of the 9 pin.

If a right-handed bowler throws the ball too hard or too far right of the intended target, then the ball either will skid too long down the lane and get into a roll too late, or it will be forced to cross more boards than it can cover on its way back to the pocket. The variable that causes the ball to skid through the front part of the lane is the heavier application of oil there, which helps protect the surface of the lane from the bruising it takes. Additionally, the amount and distribution of oil also can vary the difficulty of the game. Lanes with less oil in the front of the lane will cause the ball to hook sooner and lose energy by the time it nears the pins, while lanes with more oil in the front of the lane have precisely the opposite effect. The amount of oil applied to the lane diminishes the farther it gets from the foul line as friction intensifies between the bowling ball and the lane surface. These forces cause the ball to stop skidding and get into a roll as friction slows its forward speed and allows it to grip the lane surface. Players who naturally throw the ball harder or straighter might prefer "drier" conditions— lanes with less oil on them. Bowlers who throw the ball more slowly or hook the ball especially will appreciate more oil in the front part of the lane and even more oil down-lane as well.

On a spare leave such as the 2-4-5, the ball has come up just a bit shy of the pocket, or "light," sending the 1 pin twirling around the 2 and 4 and into the left gutter, where it slaps out the 7 pin on its way into the pit. The resulting pin action still allows for the 3, 6, 8, 9, and 10 pins to fall, leaving the 2, 4, and 5 pins remaining. The 2-4-5 is not just one of the most common spare leaves for right-handed bowlers; it also is one of the easiest to pick up for a player of Russo's ability, and everybody in the bowling alley knew it.

Russo had made a lot of mistakes over the years, but leaving an easily makeable spare standing in the 10th frame of this particular match would soon prove to be the biggest mistake of them all. No amount of effort to portray himself as just another fish would convince those who knew better that he was anything less than one of New York City's most accurate bowlers. None of them would believe it if Russo whiffed this spare. One of the side games Russo most enjoyed, in fact, was a game known as "low ball." It involved trying to bowl the lowest score on purpose, but you had to hit at least one pin on every shot. If you threw a gutter ball, it counted as a strike. Such was Russo's accuracy that he almost always bowled a 20, hitting just one corner pin—the 10 pin or the 7 pin—on each shot without touching any other pin on the deck. That required a level of skill envied even by the greatest bowlers who ever lived.

Russo would have loved to take back those careless demonstrations of his skill now, that cover he had so foolishly blown on a few lousy games of "low ball." But he could not. Stepping up to face a spare that everyone in the house had seen him make many times before, Russo assessed the situation with the cunning acuity of a born thief. He could make the spare for a win and get shot by his own backer, or miss the spare for a loss and get shot by his opponent's backer. In either case, he knew one thing for sure: Tonight would be the last night of his life.

Gangsters have a habit of simplifying decisions in people's lives, a benevolent service one of them afforded Russo when, just before he picked up his ball to throw the shot, he felt the gun of Feely's backer nudged in his belly and received his orders: "Miss this spare, and you're a dead man."

Russo grabbed his ball and stood on the approach, facing the spare that was about to bring on his demise. Then he dropped his ball to the floor, clutched his chest, and collapsed.

Russo was older than most action bowlers. Most action bowlers were in their teens or twenties. But Russo was in his forties, a guy known by neighbors as a mild-mannered family man with kids and a job. The people who populated the life Russo lived by day had no clue about this other Russo, the one who descended into the underworld of action bowling at night. And no one who populated that underworld had any idea what, exactly, Russo did during the day. Fewer could understand how a married family man could also live the life of an action bowler. When did the man sleep? Or did he sleep at all? At his age, though, the probability of a heart attack at least seemed likely enough to be taken seriously. Someone called an ambulance. Paramedics carted him off on a stretcher.

Action bowling's preeminent escape artist had decided to fake a heart attack.

And that is where tales of the most infamous heart attack ever to occur in a New York City bowling alley diverge. Some say Russo jumped out of the ambulance at the first red light. Others say he made the trip all the way to New York General before skipping out on the doctors. Most of them, though, say the gangsters either torched his car to a crisp or poured sugar in the gas tank. Nobody saw Russo's face at Avenue M Bowl for months after that, but it was not the only time Russo pulled his heart attack trick. This became the ace up his sleeve he resorted to in similarly desperate circumstances at other bowling alleys throughout the five boroughs, and it is the primary reason why those who witnessed this shyster at work never understood how he always made it out alive.

Russo may have screwed a lot of people in his day, but some of his victims asked for it. One night Russo was bowling for $1,300—a minor fortune in the early 1960s—against a kid who stepped over the foul line on almost every shot, which should result in a score of zero for that shot. With the foul lights not turned on and no foul-line judges in attendance, the kid likely figured no one would notice. Russo felt the kid was doing it on purpose to get a half-step closer to the pins. But he said nothing about it for most of the match, and continued to let the line-step happen. After leaving a 10 pin in the 10th frame, Russo picked his ball up from the rack, strolled down the entire bowling lane, laid out on his stomach, and knocked over the pin with the ball at point-blank range. After he stood up again, he walked back down the lane to the scorer's table and picked up the $1,300. Splotches of lane oil smudged his shirt.

"You fouled, I fouled!" Russo squeaked in his falsetto to his surprised opponent.

You did not have to be a hustler with a clown act to provoke the wrong man. One night, Johnny Petraglia got the idea to take Mike McGrath, his buddy from California, for a taste of the Brooklyn action. Petraglia knew McGrath was one of the most talented bowlers on the west coast. When McGrath came to visit Johnny in 1963, Johnny smelled an opportunity to score an easy buck. Both later would go on to bowl the PBA Tour. In 1963, though, they were just two more kids looking to turn the thing they loved into the thing they did for a living. Avenue M Bowl was just the place for kids like that. That, at least, was what Johnny thought.

Some who witnessed what happened next would remember gun shots fired through the ceiling. Others would remember shylocks in sharkskin suits standing at the doors with bowling balls in their hands, daring anyone to leave. No matter who told the story, though, the details made it clear that McGrath had seen enough that night—both before he walked into Avenue M Bowl and, certainly, long after he left the place alive.

Johnny got his first taste of the action in 1961 at a place in the Dyker Heights section of Brooklyn called Fortway Lanes, where the owner let him bowl for free as long as he agreed to clean tables, mop floors, and get the place ready for league after school. Johnny was not a great bowler yet on the road, but he was great at Fortway, a place loaded with shylocks on the prowl. A lot of action players had what they called their "home house," the place where they bowled most often and rarely, if ever, lost a match. If you beat a guy at his home house, though, you left the place with pockets full of money. That was the reason Fish Face's gambit with Mac and Stoop took off. Everybody wanted a piece of them at their home house because victory promised a handsome payday.

Fortway Lanes was Johnny's home house, and the shylocks knew it.

"Hey, kid," one of the shylocks said to Johnny one day, "I am going to bring some guys down here to bowl you. I will put up all the money, and you get ten percent."

Johnny was fourteen years old at the time, but he looked like he was twelve. The shylocks knew it would be easy to lure a guy into a match against him. What gambler was going to turn down an opportunity to bowl for money against a kid who looked like a grade-school altar boy? It would be some time before Johnny looked like anything more than a little kid, in fact. Even when he made the tour years later, he still cut the figure of a high-school sophomore: a body as thin as a horse hair, a gaunt face framed in thick, black sideburns that stretched from ear to chin, and a pair of horn-rimmed glasses. Long before the Petraglia name meant anything outside of Brooklyn's Fortway Lanes, it was a shylock and his body-guard's Cadillac that gave the teen his first notion of the life that awaited him.

Two weeks after Johnny got his orders at Fortway, the shy-lock's bodyguard pulled up in his Cadillac as Johnny hung out on the corner with some buddies. It was time for the match. The bodyguard carted Johnny off to Fortway, where he encountered a group of grown men twice his age with bowling balls in tow.

"This is who ya want me to bowl?" one of them said.

"Yeah, let's go," the shylock grunted. "Now."

Johnny's father was supporting a family on $63 a week. Johnny himself was making about a buck a day with his after-school gig at Fortway. But the first match he bowled that day was for $1,000. The shylock peeled off a series of $100 bills and put them on the score table. Johnny had never seen a $100 bill in his life. At first, the pressure of all that money lording over him proved a bit too much to handle. He lost the first game. Then he pondered the consequences, which, in the imagination of a fourteen-year-old, weighed just as heavily as all those $100 bills.

"This guy is gonna kill me or shoot me," Johnny thought.

But the shylock had no interest in shooting anybody. This was not some James Cagney movie; this was gambling, and the shylock was going to make money on his boy. There was nothing else to think about.

"Relax," the shylock said. "There will be a lot more games."

Johnny won the second game. Then he lost the third, but won the fourth. By then, Johnny started feeling it, and he won the fifth and sixth games. The match continued, and Johnny crushed his opposition.

"Ya did real good, kid," the shylock said. Then he peeled off a couple of those $100 bills, handed them to Johnny, and had his bodyguard take him home.

A hundred bucks went a long way in early-1960s Brooklyn, where life was as cheap as it was simple. It was a world where a nickel bought you a chocolate bar, any stoop was a front row seat to the nearest stickball game, and the pompadour was almost out of style. It also was a time when bowling alley food was about more than a greasy basket of fried cheese and a soda. Weekday specials at another Brooklyn bowling alley—Maple Lanes on 60th Street and 16th Avenue—included meals such as Greek salad, brisket, meatloaf, or chicken parmesan. In 1961, you could have ordered all four dishes at once and still hardly spent more than five bucks.

"What the hell am I gonna do with these?" Johnny asked the bodyguard. "I don't even know how to break a hundred-dollar bill!"

A few years later, Johnny hoped his biggest problem bowling with Mike McGrath would be remembering how to break a

$100 bill. When a shylock known only as "Black Sam" invited him and his friends for a night of action at Avenue M Bowl, McGrath thought of the kind of people who break things that have no business being broken—things like kneecaps and jawbones—and not the kind of people who reward talented kids from the block with more money in an afternoon than his parents made in three weeks. McGrath knew about those rumors that swirled in Brooklyn—the guns and the people who were not afraid to use them. He knew the answer to Black Sam's offer: Hell, no.

Johnny told him those rumors were overblown. He had nothing to fear, Johnny said, and told McGrath, "Mikey, you and Richie could bowl doubles there, because no one knows who you are."

That was the advantage of bringing a California kid to Brooklyn. The less familiar bowlers were with your crew, the more likely you were to find a fish. Telling McGrath he could bowl with Richie was like telling him he could bowl with God. "Richie" was Richie Hornreich, otherwise known as "The Horn," and he was the greatest action bowler in Brooklyn. Richie was Johnny's buddy. They both were growing up on the streets of Dyker Heights. Johnny knew he could count on Richie to make the trip out to Avenue M worth everyone's while.

Though everyone on the action scene agreed that Richie ranked among the greatest bowlers on the planet, and though Richie himself knew he was damn good, he did not regard his talent with much pride because bowling, for him, was merely a way to generate the income he needed to blow his money at the horse track. The ponies were Richie's weakness. He would win $5,000 at the bowling alley only to blow $6,000 at the track.

There was no shortage of tales about Richie's hunger for the thrill of another night at the races or at the craps table which he would later call his "downfall." For Richie, the point was the action itself—not bowling. He found that action by placing bets on which raindrop would slide down the bowling alley windows the fastest on rainy days, or taking a $500,000 inheritance from his father's trucking business and blowing it in Vegas in about six months. He once told a fellow action bowler named Pete Mylenki that if he found money in his pants when he took them off at night, he could not sleep.

"I gotta go empty those pockets before I can sleep," he said.

Richie possessed the unsmiling self-assurance of some Russian gangster, his jet-black bangs gushing over his tan forehead like a cresting wave. His angular jaw was shapely enough to have been chiseled out of stone, and his dark eyes seemed to stare a hole through the cameras that flashed as he posed with the first-place checks at big-time tournaments throughout the northeast. His shiny fingernails and button-down bowling shirts with stitched trim completed the manicured appearance of a guy who entered his place of work every time he walked through the doors of a bowling alley. Let the squares punch their cards between the hours of nine to five; the real money was made here on the lanes between dusk and dawn.

Anytime Richie needed to strike out in the 10th to win a match, it never crossed his mind that he might throw a bad shot. He almost never did. One night, he and another brilliant action bowler named Mike Limongello were bowling a match for quite a bit of money. Richie was up and needed a strike in the tenth to win. As he picked up his ball, he glanced at the clock on the wall, turned around to the throng of people watching the match, and said, "Cuckoo, cuckoo, cuckoo!" It was three A.M., so three cuckoos. Then he turned back around and *bang!* threw a perfect strike.

By age sixteen, Richie got invited to the World Invitational, one of the most prestigious bowling tournaments on the planet in his day and an event dominated by the biggest stars in the sport at the time—older and significantly more experienced guys like Don Carter, Dick Weber, and Carmen Salvino. But Richie did one better than merely earn an invitation: He advanced to the finals.

Clear as Richie's head may have been, his need for gambling funds bordered on a crack addict's need for a fix. Like an undisciplined blackjack player, he did not always know when to call it quits. One night, he was bowling Ernie Schlegel at a place up in White Plains, less than an hour north of New York City. For once, Richie was losing, and he was losing big. He kept trying to nudge Schlegel to raise his bet. In action bowling, that nudging could have included anything from impugning your manhood to slandering your mother. But Schlegel would not budge. He had learned his lesson in Philadelphia. So Richie pulled out a gun.

"What the fuck is that going to prove?" Schlegel said. "That I'm going to raise my bet so I can take all of your money?"

Richie, finally, called it quits.

Other times, Schlegel was not so lucky. One night Schlegel bowled Richie at a place called Ridgewood Lanes in Brooklyn with an Everest of cash piled on the score table. Richie needed at least a spare on his first shot in the tenth frame to make the money his. But on his first shot, he left the nearly impossible 7-10 split. The 7 pin is off to the farthest left-hand corner of the pin deck, while the 10 pin is off to the farthest right-hand corner. The only way to convert the split, really, is to throw the ball as hard as you can at one of the pins and hope it bangs off the sideboard or out of the pit. Then you have to hope it knocks over the other pin. Schlegel, figuring he had the game won after he saw Richie leave the dreaded 7-10, began picking up his money and counting it. Then Richie blasted the 10 pin out of the pit and watched it tomahawk the 7 pin to convert the split. Schlegel lost.

Schlegel loved seeing guys like Richie walk in after a night of big wins at the horse track because he came with loaded pockets and an unthinking willingness to throw all that money down on a match. Making money was not the point for guys like Richie. The point was making enough money to place the kind of bets that made grown men quiver. Schlegel knew that Richie was one of a few action bowlers who could beat him. He also knew that Richie may have been the better bowler some nights, but he was never the smarter bowler. Schlegel was a hustler, the kind of gambler who only bowled when he knew he had the upper hand. He knew when to bet and when to quit. He knew what amount of money to wager in a given situation and why. He knew numbers and scenarios the way a horse-race handicapper knows the names and shortcomings of jockeys. He knew when to bowl his best and when to bowl just good enough to win—just good enough, that is, to keep the other guy thinking he might have a chance if he kept trying. Richie had talent, but his thirst for gambling would always give Schlegel the upper hand.

Like those wise guys who showed up at Avenue M Bowl to seize the largesse that came with beating Mac and Stoop at their home house, sometimes Schlegel could not pass up the chance to go home with Richie's pony winnings. Some nights it worked; other times, not so much. That is how it went when you bowled Richie Hornreich. Richie was never interested in the nuances of hustling; he was interested in bowling his best at all times, no matter the opponent or the situation. If you were good enough, Richie thought, then place your bet and take your shot. For a bowler of Schlegel's caliber, it was always worth a shot—especially when Richie came back grinning from the horse track.

Looking at the other "team" that fateful night, the opportunity to bowl in a place where no one had any clue of his talent, and to partner with one of the greatest action bowlers in the world in the meantime, proved too tempting for McGrath to resist. He took Johnny up on the offer, and off to Avenue M Bowl they went. The thought would soon occur to them that it might be the last trip they would make in this world.

That night, an Avenue M regular challenged Richie to a singles match, and Richie promptly accepted. A loan shark got wind of the match and figured he would bet on bowling the way he bet on the ponies: Why put your money on the favorite when you can put it on the underdog and count on an upset? Several hundred dollars down into the match, the loan shark found, like so many before him, that he had bed against a guy who did not lose. Hornreich's opponent kept at it for a while but eventually called it quits. The Horn was just too good. And that was when the loan shark let the gun in his waistband help everyone understand how he felt about that.

"What d'ya mean, ya quit?" the shark said before taking a bowling ball in his hands, standing before the front doors of the place, and gently suggesting that the action continue.

"Nobody leaves this building until that guy bowls one more game," he said, the bowling ball clutched in one hand by his side.

"Take it easy, take it easy," someone from the loan shark's posse advised.

Those were the evening's final words of reason. The shark dropped the ball and raised a gun.

McGrath, seated within terrifying proximity to the shark and his gun, began slinking away, seat by seat, until he reached the other end of the bowling alley and tried to figure out a way to climb inside the wall. All those rumors Johnny told him were not true about Brooklyn had turned out to be truer than he had imagined. This would be one of those nights when rumor and reality got a little too cozy with one another. Hopefully, it would also be a night McGrath would live to tell about. Right now, he was not so sure.

The kids bowled another game, all right—a couple of terrified 120s riddled with open frames as they attempted to master the underappreciated skill of bowling while simultaneously pissing themselves.

"Ya little prick," Black Sam's bodyguard told the shark, shoving the mouth of a gun in the back of his head. "For what you did to those kids, I should take that gun and shove it up your ass."

The bodyguard turned to Black Sam and asked, "What do you want me to do?"

"Just give me the piece," Black Sam advised before looking up at the shark and taking his gun. "Now get the fuck out of here."

"You said we were gonna be safe," McGrath squeaked on the way home from the back of Black Sam's Cadillac. "I will never come back here again."

Black Sam turned to McGrath, his bodyguard behind the wheel.

"If you open your mouth again, I'll leave you out in the street right here and you'll *really* see what it's like!"

It was four A.M. in a part of town where a west-coast kid like Mike McGrath might have looked like food to the locals. He shut his mouth, a precocious act of wisdom to which he probably owed his life.

Sadly, that sort of wisdom might have helped preserve the life of a local tough guy known as Mattie. Mattie lacked as much in wisdom as he possessed in brawn, and this flaw in his character soon spelled the demise of the action at Avenue

M. Mattie ran with a bike gang out of Coney Island that had a reputation for robbery and the guns and fists they used to carry it out. People knew him as the type of guy who could slap your back and laugh one minute and crush your face with a single blow the next. So when he broke in on a card game at Al Rosa's apartment one night with a mask and a shotgun looking to clean the place out, nobody uttered a word of protest, even those who knew it was him. The mask could conceal Mattie's face, but not his voice. He made everyone strip to their bare asses. Then he took their clothes and their money and ran.

But Mattie never did his due diligence about who he came after, and by the end of 1963, he crossed the kind of guy you did not run from: a member of the Gallo gang. Mattie, strung out on drugs and booze, thought it would be a good idea to make fun of Gallo while the gangster had a drink at a local bar. What a big mouth on this guy, Gallo thought. Gallo was the kind of guy who knew how to take care of people with big mouths. One night two Cadillacs pulled up to the bowling alley. Four guys in suits got out and went looking for Mattie. They found him, of course, in the lounge upstairs. They asked him to step outside. It was the kind of question that Mattie always eagerly answered in the affirmative to ensure everyone understood he feared no one. It was the last question he would answer in his life. The four gangsters took Mattie out into the street and each fired one bullet into his mouth. *This is what we do with guys who have big mouths*, their action seemed to say.

The cops heard that message as loudly as anyone and circled the premises for weeks. Not surprisingly, the proximity to police officers made underage gamblers uneasy, and soon the gambling den that originated with Fish Face and his bait, Mac and Stoop, returned to the days of hushed nights and slow business. As would be the case with many bowling alleys that became hotbeds of action bowling, the Mattie incident ensured that the action at Avenue M Bowl died just as it seemed to have reached its zenith. The circus that was action bowling needed a new home. It would be no time at all before it found one.

3
CENTRAL

The circus moved to a place where even the street names had guns in them. Gun Post Lanes was on East Gun Hill Road in the Bronx. A huge expanse of French windows flanked the front doors, making it impossible to conceal the debauchery within. This architectural quirk would soon become the source of yet another upheaval in the action bowling scene. Gun Post was a two-story bowling alley with forty-eight lanes and a manager everybody called "Skee," a guy who possessed the same acumen for promotion that made Fish Face a genius. Skee had come up with a game he called "Boomerang" in which bowlers would toss some money into a pot, throw one frame on each of twelve lanes, and the top two or three bowlers would divide the cash. Then they would return to the first pair of lanes and do it again. As entries went up, so did the money. Soon, the big boys started coming around. Saturday nights at Gun Post saw action on every pair of lanes, upstairs and down, beginning at 1 A.M. and persisting through dawn. The carpets gave off a reek of gangsters' cigars as gamblers penciled their debts into the score table from one end of the alley to the other, every lane crowded with a shouting rush of gamblers looking to get their bets in.

The craps games that had flourished around the lockers at Avenue M now found their home in the men's restroom at Gun Post. Gamblers who came to the party a bit late and found the men's room filled to capacity with craps players took the action to the ladies' room instead. So acute was their addiction to gambling, in fact, that one bowler known as "Psycho Dave" once arrived directly from a wedding and bowled in his tux. Another bowler in his early twenties, Mike Ginsberg, was surprised when his parents appeared just after dawn, imploring him to leave because they had a family road trip to get on with. Ginsberg refused. So his father muttered something about the bums he kept for company, then went back out to the car, dumped Ginsberg's clothes into the street, and left him behind.

The whole cast of characters the cops scared away from Avenue M made Gun Post their new haunt. Iggy Russo with his lead-filled bowling pins and his clown act. The Kangaroo and The Leaper. Freddy the Ox. But Gun Post saw the emergence of new names, too, such as One Finger Benny, who could bowl 180 using just one finger in a lighter bowling ball—eight pounds—and usually made money doing it; Ira "The Whale" Katz, as famous for his girth as Freddy The Ox; or Bobby Pancakes who, rumor had it, was afflicted with an unending appetite for pancakes. Others wore their jobs like nametags. There was Mike the Cab Driver, Tony the Milkman, Morris the Mailman, or Bill "Pepsi" Vanacore, who worked for the Pepsi-Cola company.

The names may have sounded funny to some people, but few would dare laugh, especially not a bowler known as

"Goldfinger," who earned his Bond villain-esque name in a way Bond himself would have relished. Goldfinger got his nickname because of the bowling ball he used. Brunswick, one of the main manufacturers of bowling balls, was making a series of balls called "Crown Jewels." One, called the "Gold Crown Jewel," was flecked with flakes of gold. Some thought it was real gold, while others insisted the flecks were nothing more than sequins or glittery, plastic specks. That was Goldfinger's ball of choice, and he made enough money with it to justify the extravagance. Unlike most action bowlers, who were natives of New York City or New England, Goldfinger actually lived in Florida. So talented a hustler was Goldfinger that he made enough to hustle for a few days throughout the five boroughs and then buy himself a plane ticket back to Florida. Then he would board a plane a few weeks later and head up to New York to do it again.

Goldfinger was so good, in fact, that even Ernie Schlegel learned a few tips from the man. One night, Schlegel was bowling Bill Daley, who was as renowned for his bowling ability as he was for his cunning as a gambler. Daley drubbed Schlegel for the first three games. Schlegel's backers started getting worried. Then Schlegel remembered something. He had heard that Goldfinger had beaten Daley at this same bowling alley weeks earlier, and he knew also that the only line Goldfinger could play on the lane with any success was the 10 board or the second arrow, a portion of the lane known to bowlers colloquially as "the track." That part of the lane became known as "the track" because it is a part of the lane most right-handed bowlers commonly play. Consequently, the track becomes worn down over time, causing the oil there to dry up or become depleted more quickly than on any other part of the lane. Just as a guy with a snow shovel digs a path from the front door of his house out to the street in a winter storm, a bowling ball carves a path through the oil on the lane that provides a reliable avenue to the pocket. Ridges of oil to the left and right of the track essentially cradle the ball and guide it toward the pocket as it proceeds down the lane. Bowlers who speak of "playing the track" mean they are taking advantage of this quirk in the lane conditions. The track can enable a capable bowler to strike at will for hours on end.

Unlike Goldfinger, Daley was playing the extreme outside portion of the lane to the right of the 5 board, a strategy known in bowling as "playing the gutter." He was drubbing Schlegel from out there. Schlegel decided to move in to the 10 board and play the the track like Goldfinger had. It worked; he beat Daley seven games in a row. He beat Daley so soundly, in fact, that the shylock loaning Daley money to keep him in the match ended up running out of money himself. In a twist of fate perhaps unprecedented in action bowling history, the shylock, for once, was the one asking for cash. He asked Schlegel if he would spot him some. By then, Schlegel had made enough money. Rather than spot the shylock to continue the match, he took his winnings and headed out to beat the rush-hour traffic.

As might be expected of a guy with a nickname like "Goldfinger," however, ultimately he proved to be a bit too cute for his own good. He tried to cheat the kind of guys who cheated for a living—the shylocks and backers who flocked to Gun Post as surely as the action bowlers did. Goldfinger had a reputation for lodging lead in his bowling ball to give it more "side weight." He did this through a process called "plugging." It involved drilling a hole in the bowling ball, embedding lead or pouring mercury into the hole, and then topping it off with a liquid that hardened overnight like glue, trapping the lead or mercury inside. According to the crooks and shysters whose income depended on the extent of their mastery over the various measures of deception, side weight turned the ball so sharply toward the headpin that it obliterated the pocket with an authority no ordinary bowling ball could possibly achieve. He made a lot of money this way. Steve Harris, who ran his own pro shop at 4840 Broadway on the corner of Broadway and Academy in upper Manhattan, would buy mercury from the drugstore and use it to "plug" bowling balls. He did the same with lead sinkers he would get from bait and tackle shops, but he insisted it was impossible to control bowling balls after manipulating them. The density of lead or mercury gave the bowling ball more hitting power—the kind of advantage Goldfinger sought. One bowler, Al Sergeant, unknowingly became a beneficiary of this practice. He bowled with a white towel draped over his shoulder and a cigar pinned between two fingers in his left hand while he threw the ball with his right. Sergeant's ability as a spare shooter earned him recognition as the "king of the clean game"; he averaged about a 189 throwing his ball straight up the 15th board, rarely missing the pocket and never missing a spare. He threw the ball with so little angle and power, however, that he rarely carried pocket hits for strikes; he left a lot of 8-10 splits, 5-7 splits, 5-10 splits, and 10 pins. One night, a guy named Eddie Fenton, who owned a pro shop on Broadway and Dungan Place in Inwood, removed Sergeant's ball from his locker, took it to his shop, and plugged it with lead. Sergeant, known to be as honest a man as he was accurate a bowler, never would have participated in the practice himself. But the ball he removed from his locker the next day made him a new bowler. Those 8-10 splits he left before now were just 10 pins he converted for spares; those pocket 10 pins he left now were strikes. If Sergeant had any idea what was going on, he never let on.

Goldfinger hoped to enjoy some of the magic Fenton had bestowed upon Al Sergeant. He had just won four consecutive matches with a loaded ball when a group of gangsters betting on his opponent noticed the same peculiarity in the movement of his bowling ball. Unfortunately for Goldfinger, the gangsters were not interested in giving him a snappy nickname for the move; they were interested in making him pay for it.

"He's throwin' a loaded ball," one of the gangsters growled as he pulled his cigar out of his face.

One of the gangster's goons took Goldfinger's ball back to the pro shop to check it out. He weighed the ball and found that it had half an ounce of extra side weight. So they grabbed Goldfinger, laid him on the ground, held his bowling ball high over their heads, and smashed it down on his bowling hand. The blow blasted the bones in Goldfinger's hand into so many little pieces they could have been used as mulch. Everybody in the action bowling scene got the message: it may help to load your bowling ball, but having your hand pounded to a pulp by gangsters did not sound like fun. His next trip back to Florida would be the last time he headed back home after a night of action up north; he never bowled again.

But mercury plugs and lead sinkers from the local bait and tackle shop ranked among the crudest deceits employed by the more refined practitioners of hustling. Like Avenue M Bowl, Gun Post provided the stage on which many of action bowling's most inimitable characters performed with subtlety and style.

Ralph Engan, who then was nearly forty while most other action bowlers were in their teens and twenties, was renowned for his smooth delivery and deadly accuracy. To beat Ralph Engan—the elder statesman of the action bowling scene—was to beat the best. Being known as "the best" was a double-edged sword, however; bragging rights are great, but ultimately they are only as good as the money that comes with your next win. It is awfully hard to win when no one can find the courage to bowl you, and that is why con men like Iggy Russo were on to something. Why blow people away with your skill when you can fool them into thinking you had no skill at all? Engan was no Iggy Russo; he wanted to bowl you man to man and beat you with his best. But he also wanted to make money, and after spending too many nights sitting through hours of action waiting for challengers who never came, even Engan had to use some wiles. Sometimes he headed out to bowling alleys beyond the five boroughs, places where he could be reasonably sure people did not know of him. He would plant his bowling ball among the regular house balls on the ball racks. Then he would feign cluelessness as he fumbled through them while his prospective opponent prepared to wager any amount of money on a match against a bum who owned no ball of his own. Engan always seemed to find exactly the same ball on the rack—his own. And when he did, the match was his before anyone threw a shot.

Engan, in fact, was the guy who first tutored Ernie Schlegel in the art of the out-and-out hustle. One night Schlegel kept hearing Engan complain about how tired he was, and a chance to seize the largesse that surely would accompany a victory over the great Ralph Engan was one Schlegel could not pass up. Ralph bowled Schlegel all night, telling him how tired he was all along, until Schlegel passed out from exhaustion. Engan won big. It was a lesson Schlegel never forgot.

But by the mid-1960s, Schlegel himself was dishing out far more lessons than he received. He was no longer the green rookie who scoured Philadelphia for fish. Some even considered him the greatest action bowler they had ever seen. Now in his early twenties, he was bowling every night of the week and making more money in a month than his parents made in a year. He had sharpened his game to the point where he felt ready to take a shot on the PBA Tour. For now, however, he still was catching enough fish to be content with his life as an action bowler. The tour would come, but only when he found himself having to resort to Engan's antics to get somebody to bowl him. Schlegel did not mind rubbing bourbon behind his ears or faking the gout now and then, but when things got desperate enough for him to pretend he had never seen a bowling ball in his life, well, that was when he would know the time to move on had come. Schlegel considered himself a businessman before he considered himself a bowler. For him, Gun Post was a kind of crooked accountant's office he would happily occupy as long as the money kept coming in. As the gamblers of Gun Post would learn, Schlegel's version of a businessman was one who feared nobody and stopped at nothing to protect his cut.

One night Schlegel had a score to settle with a man named Psycho Dave, who had conned him out of $600 in a game of Gin Rummy. Psycho Dave had trounced Schlegel and his buddy Stevie, only for them to find out later that Psycho Dave had been cheating. So Schlegel took Stevie out looking for Psycho Dave one night. Stevie, a scrappy guy who stood 6'1" and 190 lbs., was the kind of buddy you bring out when you needed to issue non-refusable offers to those who owed you. They found Psycho Dave up in the Bronx at a place called All-Star Lanes. Stevie walked up to Psycho.

"Where's my money?" he asked.

"What money?" Psycho Dave replied.

Then Stevie round-housed him hard enough to send him flying over a ball return.

"I am only gonna ask you once," Stevie told him. "And that was it. Now, where's my money?"

Psycho Dave may have been psycho, but there is something about a swift fist to the face that restores sanity. Psycho Dave knew exactly what Stevie was talking about. He proved sane enough to pay up on the spot.

The kind of company Schlegel kept was the kind that played a little game he liked to call "You hurt me, and they shoot you," which was a pretty pointed reference to the mobsters who liked to gamble on him. But he had other means of protecting himself against the unsavory elements any sworn gambler had to run with on occasion. Years later, sports writer Herm Weiskopf would document the kind of garb Schlegel donned as a kid to keep the street gangs off his back: "He was fond of dressing in black stovepipe pants, a white silk shirt, an iridescent raincoat and high Roman heels," Weiskopf wrote. "He also sported a Mohican haircut and carried an umbrella with its tip filed to a point." What fool would step up to a kid who dressed that way in places where the people were as threatening as the weapons their coats concealed? Only the craziest of the crazy, and that alone made most folks steer clear of him.

But if they did step up, Schlegel concealed his own assort- ment of weapons. One night he spotted some talent up at a place on 168th Street and Webster Avenue in the Bronx called Webster Lanes, a twenty-year-old kid out of Long Island named Mike Limongello. "Lemon," as he was known, already was the king of the Long Island action scene. Nobody beat Lemon out there. Now he was making a name for himself in the five boroughs, where he heard he could make some real money. It would not be long before people uttered Lemon's name in the same breath as guys like Schlegel, Richie Hornreich, or Johnny Petraglia.

Lemon rivaled Schlegel's flare for fashion as much as he rivaled his ability. At a ceremony in which he accepted the New York Metropolitan Bowler of the Year award in 1965, he sported a ducktail hairdo slathered in Pomade, a sharp, ivory-white suit with a flowered lapel, and a black bowtie that sparkled in the flash of reporters' cameras. He could just as easily have been standing in for Frank Sinatra at a Rat Pack gig as accepting a bowling award. His remarkably huge, green eyes earned him the nickname "Banjo Eyes" on the action scene; he always had the look of a doe staring directly into the headlights of an oncoming truck.

Schlegel's concern was money, not fashion, and he saw plenty of it in this brash bulldog from the Island who almost never missed the pocket and took on all comers for any amount of money, anywhere, anytime. One guy who could have told Schlegel about Lemon was Richie Hornreich, who already had clashed with Lemon at a Long Island house called Garden City Bowl. Hornreich was bowling league there one night when in walked Lemon and his crew, looking for action. The Horn gladly supplied it, but quickly fell behind as Lemon crushed him 220-170 in the first game, then did it again in the second. Then Hornreich got an idea.

"Mikey, I got nothing on this pair," he said. "If you want to keep bowling, we need to move to a different pair."

So move to a different pair of lanes they did, and the action exploded. Lemon started losing shooting 250s to The Horn's 260s. But the action would not last for long that night. Just as Hornreich thought he was on his way to cleaning Lemon out, his thumb ripped open and began gushing blood. It was time for another idea. The Horn always had another idea, especially when it came to money.

"Mikey, I can't bowl, but I'm not gonna quit on ya," Hornreich said. "Bet whatever you want and I will bowl one last game, blood and all."

Just in case Lemon thought he was kidding, Hornreich put down $2,500. Then he threw the first ten strikes in a row. On the second ball in the tenth frame, he left a 10 pin. Lemon had started the game with a spare and then strung the next nine consecutive strikes. Hornreich finished with a 279, easily enough to beat most players. Most players, that is, with the exception of Mike Limongello. Lemon needed at least the first two strikes in the 10th frame to win. He did one better: He blasted three perfect strikes, and the money was his.

That was the thing about Lemon; he was more action bowler than hustler. All he knew how to do was bowl his best every time he hit the lanes. And Lemon's best almost always was better than anyone else's. Schlegel, on the other hand, was a hustler. He only bowled well enough to win and rarely more than that. That was how the smart hustlers preserved the air of vulnerability they needed to attract challengers. Here was the goldmine Schlegel had been dreaming about—a doubles partner he could count on to blast the pocket all night long while Schlegel did just enough to keep them ahead. Why bother bowling better than 180 or 190 when the guy you were bowling with could bowl 250s and 260s just as effortlessly? Schlegel knew where to take his new partner in business: Gun Post Lanes.

"If you really want some action," Schlegel told Lemon, "come to Gun Post Lanes in the Bronx. Bring anybody you want, and bring lots of money, because there will be people there from all over the place and you can get any match you want."

The best way for Schlegel to size up Lemon's talent was first to bowl the man himself. So Schlegel teamed up with a good bowler from the Bronx named Johnny Masarro, who once bowled for the New York Gladiators team in the short-lived National Bowling League. Unlike the Professional Bowlers Association, which focused on a singles-competition concept fashioned after professional golf, the NBL focused on team competition inspired by professional leagues in other sports such as football, baseball, basketball, and hockey. NBL players would earn annual salaries just like pros in any pro sports league.

Bowling arenas were constructed as homes for some NBL teams. Texas oilman J. Curtis Sanford, the visionary behind the establishment of college football's Cotton Bowl in 1937, pumped $3 million into the construction of the Bronco Bowl to house his NBL team, the Dallas Broncos. With 72 lanes, the establishment was the largest bowling alley in the country at the time. Another arena called Thunder Bowl—home of the Detroit Thunderbirds—went up in Allen Park, Michigan, with stadium-style seating for spectators capable of holding thousands of fans. Similarly ambitious digs went up in Bloomington, Minnesota, and Forth Worth to house the Twin Cities Skippers and the Fort Worth Panthers respectively. Elsewhere, famed theaters such as the Midland in Kansas City and the Paramount in Omaha were transformed into bowling arenas. Those venues became home to the Kansas City Stars and the Omaha Packers. Masarro's New York Gladiators sought to make their home atop Grand Central Station, "where it had hoped to perch like a city pigeon," as one 1961 *Sports Illustrated* story about the NBL's inception put it. Instead, in a turn of events that foreshadowed the ill-fated league's demise, they ended up 20 miles away at a stadium in Totowa, New Jersey. Other NBL teams included the San Antonio Cavaliers as well as California's Fresno Bombers and the Los Angeles Toros.

The NBL barely lasted through its first season, from October, 1961 through July, 1962, when then-commissioner Ed Tobolowski officially declared the league defunct. The NBL failed to land a much hoped-for television contract and never lured the likes of Dick Weber or Don Carter—then the rock stars of the sport—away from the PBA and other, more lucrative endorsements and commitments. Those names might have helped the NBL garner the star power it sorely needed to succeed. Weber and Carter made as much money bowling as pro athletes made in any other sport in those days, including marquee stars such as baseball's Yogi Berra, Stan Musial or Mickey Mantle. Rumors swirled about bribes offered by NBL executives, one of whom allegedly tried to propitiate Don Carter by offering him a pig farm. Carter must not have cared much for pigs; he never did bowl in the NBL.

Masarro's participation in the NBL meant he learned as much about great bowling as he learned about great characters even before he descended into New York City's action bowling underworld. The NBL may have failed to attract Weber and Carter, but it still boasted competitors who were as dazzling in their skill as they were in personality—future Hall of Famers such as Carmen Salvino, Steve Nagy, Billy Golembiewski, Joe Joseph, Therm Gibson, Ed Lubanski and others. None of them were as inimitable as "Buzz" Fazio out of Akron, Ohio—Buzz being short for the name given him by his Sicilian parents, Basilino. Fazio converted the nearly impossible 7-10 split not once, but twice, on his way to winning the prestigious Masters tournament in 1955. He defeated two tumors, survived a car wreck that cost him his spleen and nearly a leg, and a barber who accidentally sliced his bowling thumb down to the bare bone while wiping off a shaving blade in his lap one day. (Fazio somehow finished the final stretch of the renowned All-Star tournament anyway.) Fazio's antics included leaping to click his heels together in mid-air after throwing a great shot and crashing down to his hands and knees at the foul line to wish his ball where he needed it to go. Fazio fell so in love with bowling as a 16-year-old kid in Akron that he would slip down the coal chute of a place called Butchel's Recreation before dawn, feel around in the dark of the building's cellar to find his way into the place, then set up some pins for himself and bowl alone before his friends arrived.

After banging heads with guys like Fazio in the NBL, no amount of skill or bluster was going to rattle Masarro in a crack-of-dawn doubles match at Gun Post Lanes in the Bronx, and Schlegel knew it. Lemon bowled with a guy named Phil

Lamenzo, and the match was on. Lamenzo was a decent bowler, but a lot of guys were decent bowlers until their wallets told them otherwise. Lemon liked to play a particular part of the lane out in Long Island—the third arrow, closer to the pocket, where his accuracy served him well with a straight shot up the 15th board and into the pocket. Out in the Bronx, though, Lemon was learning the hard way that the inside shot he liked out on the Island didn't play so well in New York City. There are many reasons why the lane conditions might be different in one part of town versus another. Sometimes the lane surface was older than in other bowling alleys; over time, the wear of many games and harsh weather—the stultifying humidity and heat of a New York City summer, or the brutal cold snaps and blizzards in the winter months—would cause grooves, warps, or other idiosyncrasies. Or the lanes at some bowling centers might have topographical quirks—subtle grooves, slopes or humps in the lane perceptible only to the most observant eye. And even then, you really had to know what you were looking for. Sometimes the ball's reaction as it proceeded down the lane would tell the story. If no one could get their bowling ball to hook on one lane, and everyone always had trouble throwing it straight on another, no matter what time of day or how much oil had been put down, that could say as much about the composition of the lane as it might about a given bowler's ability. A slight downward slope in the lane, however imperceptible, would increase the speed of the ball which had the same effect as throwing the ball too hard; the ball is less likely to hook as much as a bowler would like it to. The harder a bowler throws the ball, the farther the ball will skid down the lane before it gets into a roll and then, finally, hooks back toward the pocket—or "grabs" the lane, as some bowlers say. Just as a downward slope in a lane's topography causes the ball to accelerate and therefore hook less than desired, an incline in a lane's topography, however slight, slows down the bowling ball, which may cause the ball to get into a roll sooner than the bowler would like and therefore hook too much.

Schlegel's understanding of these variables was one of the things that made him great. He memorized the contours and idiosyncrasies of every lane he bowled on throughout the five boroughs. He knew every warped board, every topographical quirk, every blemish and bend. Because he bowled in a different bowling alley every night of the week, he accumulated an immense store of knowledge that he used to his advantage.

Action bowlers commonly insisted on bowling on a specific pair of lanes if they were going to agree to a match; if the opponent refused, the match was off. If he agreed, he soon would learn why his adversary wanted to bowl on that particular pair of lanes—because he knew those lanes better than anyone in the house. Sometimes, though, a bowler who agreed to bowl on another player's favorite pair and beat him could end up winning a lot of money, because a bowler who thinks he cannot be beaten on a particular pair of lanes is a bowler who is more prone to betting like a fool. Schlegel knew which pair he loved in every bowling alley he entered, and he made sure to bowl only on pairs that gave him an upper hand. That is an advantage gamblers did not have at the racetrack or in a game of cards. You don't get to decide if it's going to rain the day of a horse race and affect the outcome by muddying the track, just as you don't get to decide when you will get a royal flush—unless, of course, you're the Iggy Russo of poker. But action bowlers often did get to decide what pair of lanes they would agree to bowl on for money, which also was to decide implicitly the lane conditions on which the match would commence. That is an advantage any gambler gladly would take.

Sometimes these idiosyncrasies were manufactured by con men who deliberately manipulated the lanes to their advantage. In the 1950s, when lane surfaces were coated with lacquer, some bowlers would place a horse hair on the seventeenth board—the board leading directly into the pocket—and paste it to the lane's surface with a coating of lacquer. If you threw the ball straight and weak enough, it would catch that horse hair and be guided directly into the pocket for a strike. Such schemers also sometimes manipulated the approaches as well as the lanes. If a bowler noticed his opponent's sliding foot landed on the eleventh board, for instance, he would slide hard on the eleventh board with the rubber heel of his sliding shoe, leaving a streak on the approach that would cause his opponent to stick. When a bowler would stick once, it would be in his head for the rest of the match. Take out a bowler's footwork and you take out his entire game.

For whatever reason, the lanes in New York City did not play the way they played out on the Island, and Lemon was struggling to adjust. Schlegel was noticing that, too. But, like any good businessman, he waited until after he had pocketed some of Lemon's money before advising him of the problem. Lemon struggled just enough for Schlegel and Masarro to come out on top.

Even as he struggled, Lemon bowled well enough to keep things close. Then Masarro, who himself was a hell of a bowler, took on Lemon in a singles match. Lemon, still decent to figure out how to play the lanes in a house he had never bowled in before, eventually lost the match. Schlegel was betting on Masarro the whole time, knowing Lemon did not stand a chance playing the third arrow at Gun Post. Then Masarro got greedy and cut Schlegel out of the betting. He wanted all the money to himself. That was all Schlegel needed to hear to know it was time to let Lemon in on the little secrets of how the big boys played the lanes in New York City.

But first he tried to warn Masarro.

"Wait a minute! John, I brought these guys here! I gotta get a piece of the action," Schlegel said. "What the fuck are you doing?"

Masarro wasn't having it, so Schlegel turned to Lemon.

"Hey, can I bet on you?" Schlegel asked him.

Lemon looked at him like he was nuts.

"Bet on me?" Lemon said. "Why? I can't find a shot at this place."

"Hey, this is action. I bet on whoever I think has a chance to win," Schlegel said. "I brought you here. They just cut me out, and I'm pissed. So now I'm betting on you. Now listen, you're playing the lanes too far inside. Why don't you move outside a little bit, closer to the second arrow, around the ten board, and play the lanes there. See what happens."

Schlegel knew damned well what would happen—he was coaching Lemon to play that trusty "track" he himself manipulated against Bill Daley. The part of the lane that made Lemon money at bowling alleys in his native Long Island might not work as well at bowling alleys in New York City, but Lemon's talent enabled him to play the track as expertly as anyone in all of New York. Once he got Lemon lined up, Masarro, good as he was, had no chance against a guy with the kind of talent Lemon possessed. Schlegel also knew that Lemon possessed the very intangibles that made him great himself; Lemon had those things people call "it factors." He had the drive, the determination, the work ethic, the obsession, the streak of vengeance in his cool and calculated resolve when circumstances demanded that he either make a great shot or lose everything. One man's talent is another's killer instinct; Lemon, like Schlegel, had enough of both to spare some. If he found himself bowling a guy who was as talented, or a guy who had him nailed on a particularly difficult pair of lanes, Lemon was the kind of competitor who willed his way to victory somehow. For guys like Schlegel and Lemon, competition was a matter of pride and self-respect. It was a matter of believing that no one was better than they were. It was a matter of knowing that as surely as they knew their own names.

Lemon moved outside as Schlegel advised and proceeded to crush Masarro. Game after game, bet after bet, Masarro had no answer. The real winner, as always, was Schlegel. Schlegel had made lots of money betting on Masarro earlier; now he was making money betting the other way and advising Masarro's opponent. Masarro knew it, and he let his fists show Schlegel how he felt about it. He took a swing at him.

Schlegel ducked. Then he pulled a knife.

"You do that again and I'll have to fuckin' stab you," Schlegel said.

Masarro shut his mouth.

"Yeah," Schlegel said. "What do you think, I come here with fuckin' nothing?"

That knife Schlegel pulled when circumstances called for it would eventually land him in more trouble than he cared to manage. For now, though, it was one way to make sure he kept his money in the same place where Fish Face preferred to keep his—in his pocket. After that night, Schlegel took Lemon all over New York City, bowling as his doubles partner everywhere they went, and winning at every turn. Lemon was Schlegel's secret weapon precisely because he was a weapon few had seen before. To New York City kids, bowling out on Long Island was like bowling out on Mars. It took time for people in New York City to figure out what Lemon was all about. And when they did, as was the case with Ralph Engan and would be the case with Schlegel himself, they ran out of fish. Nobody was willing to take them on. The gig was up, but the $3,000 they made in the meantime easily was enough to make their time as a duo worthwhile, brief as it may have been. In 1965, $3,000 was an embarrassment of riches to anybody (roughly $22,000 today), no less a couple of street kids barely out of their teens.

The status Gun Post Lanes enjoyed as the gathering place for gamblers and gangsters from far and wide proved just as brief as Schlegel's partnership with Lemon. Wherever the action found a new home, the cops who cleaned out the old one always seemed to come around again. The night they came around to Gun Post Lanes was one no witness would forget.

The lights that glowed through those French windows flanking the front of the place caught the attention of a couple of plainclothes cops on the beat. There is something about the sight of so many teenagers waving fistfuls of cash that catches a cop's attention, especially when it happens to be four o'clock in the morning. One cop took a seat at the lunch counter next to Johnny Kourabas while the other had a look around. Kourabas knew there was something about the guy that didn't belong; this was not your usual gambler waiting to arrange a match. Then he heard the other cop advising people to make sure they kept their hands nice and high in the air, and Kourabas knew the gig was up.

The comprehensiveness with which the cops dismantled the debauchery at Gun Post was that of someone who empties half a can of Raid on a roach and then steps on it to kill it again. The cops swept the place clean of cash. Then they handcuffed a scorekeeper to the table into which he scratched the names and debts of all in attendance, unscrewed the table from the floor, and took both down to the station as evidence. It was the last night of action Gun Post ever saw—and the beginning of an era's demise.

Action bowling took its final breath at a place called Central Lanes in Yonkers, just north of New York City. Central Lanes was a long, low building that housed fifty-two lanes straight across and an enclosed coffee shop with fifteen stools and windows overlooking the parking lot. A frenetic scene buzzed in the air of that coffee shop when the action got thick late at night. Hustlers, con artists, and gamblers were brought together by matchmakers who would arrange matches as bets came in from all directions through shouts and fists full of cash. The bowlers drew their lane numbers from a pillbox full of numbers someone shook, and the match would be held on the lanes whose numbers were drawn. To adrenaline-hungry kids with dollar signs for pupils, this truly was a paradise straight out of their wildest dreams.

Gamblers trying to find the place for the first time could count on any number of signs that they had found it. They might spot the legion of kids pitching dice for cash in the parking lot. They might look through the windows enclosing the pool room at one end of the building and see the high-stakes games of eight ball raging inside. They might notice a parking lot bloated with the cars of fellow gamblers in the middle of the night and have a hard time finding a spot themselves. And if some nor'easter happened to be dumping another blast of snow over Yonkers in winter, that, too, failed to deter the circus. It was not uncommon to see cars twirling down the icy streets toward the bowling alley. Gamblers would sooner leave their cars lodged in snow piles in the middle of the street than miss a night of action at Central. A snowplow could gnash their cars into little foil balls for all they cared; Central was a place where those who placed their bets wisely could leave with enough cash to buy new ones anyway.

It also was a place where bowlers who placed bets with money borrowed from shylocks sometimes needed to be reminded of the penalties. No one at Central Lanes received that reminder more clearly than a kid known as "Checkbook" Al. Al was a skinny kid with glasses in his early twenties whose nickname said it all. At Central Lanes, he was known as much for writing bad checks as he was known for his bowling. He nearly became known for dying, too, after he borrowed money off a feared, Jewish shylock known as Maxie. Maxie was a stocky guy with fat fingers who spoke with a voice that sounded like it came from somewhere in the bottom of his gut, and he always sat the wrong way in a chair with his chest leaning up against the back of it. At any given moment kids could hear him grunting offers from behind the lanes at bowlers whose luck was running thin.

"Joe, how much you need," he'd say in his husky growl and Brooklyn accent. "Mikey, how much you need?"

Bowlers would walk up to Maxie and say "Gimme five," and Maxie would snap out five crisp $100 bills. His rate was ten percent per week, and everything went fine—as long as you paid him back. The smart ones paid him back right away. One night, Schlegel borrowed about $1,200, then won that much and more in a match and paid back Maxie on the spot. That was how you handled shylocks like Maxie if you knew what was good for you.

Maxie always wore a rumpled suit. He had a balding bull's head of gray hair and always kept a lit Camel pinned between two tobacco-stained fingertips. Many presumed him to be a gangster, but he always carried himself with an avuncular manner that disarmed those who otherwise might have feared him. The shylocks knew as much about catching flies with honey as the hustlers did. You didn't get customers by scaring them anymore than you caught fish by letting on how good you were. Even when some customers needed to be scared because they hadn't paid up, Maxie issued his threats gently enough that it was almost possible to believe he was kidding.

"You don't want me to have to hurt you," Maxie would tell them.

But Maxie wasn't kidding, especially not the day he sent one of his goons to find Checkbook Al. When the goon found him inside the coffee house at Central Lanes, everyone knew from that moment forward that Maxie never was kidding. Checkbook Al rushed in one day as kids hunched over their hamburgers at the counter. He pestered each of them for money.

"Hey, ya got forty bucks?" he asked.

"Get the fuck away from me," one kid told him. "You owe *me* money!"

Then the goon arrived. He was a ruddy-faced moose of a man with broad shoulders who looked like he played left tackle for the New York Giants. The strange thing was that as tough as the guy looked, he nonetheless was wearing a bright pink, fuzzy, pullover sweater. No one quite understood what to make of that bizarre detail.

The goon walked up to Checkbook Al.

"OK, your time is up," he said. "You got Max's money?"

"No, I don't have it," Checkbook told him.

The goon grabbed Checkbook with one arm and hoisted him up in the air. The two paused nose-to-nose for a second, Checkbook dangling limply in the air. Then the goon tossed him like a football. It was like he had shot the kid out of a cannon. Checkbook went blasting through the windows of the coffee shop and out into the parking lot in a hail of shattered glass. That was all it took to separate the rest of the crowd from their hamburgers. Everybody promptly got up and left. No one looked back. They did not even look left or right. The point was to get the hell out of there. No one bothered to see if Checkbook was alive or dead, and nobody ever talked about it.

That was how it went when you took money off a shylock. You weren't just borrowing money; you were also borrowing time. That night Maxie returned to his backwards chair with his suit and his Camel, barking offers to those in need as though nothing had happened.

Many bowlers sent their opponents off to borrow from Maxie more often than they would have liked. Few bowlers put people in that uncomfortable position more frequently than Schlegel. By the time Central Lanes became established as action bowling's new gathering place, Schlegel exhibited the raging brazenness of a gambler who knew he couldn't lose. He sported a T-shirt that said "World's Greatest Bowler," pounding his chest like a gorilla and challenging all comers. Gobs of Vaseline from his duck's ass hairdo melted down his face on muggy summer nights. The proprietor of Central Lanes kept a giant trophy on display beside the check-in counter in front of lanes 17 and 18; it was reserved for the first bowler to shoot a 300 game at Central Lanes. Schlegel claimed the trophy in a match against a brilliant, seventeen-year-old talent named Dewey Blair.

Blair was the phantom of the action bowling scene. Everybody had heard about this high school kid nobody could beat, but no one ever saw him. Blair's home house was a place called Dutchess County Lanes, about 50 miles north of New York City. There, he took on, and nearly always beat, all challengers. He made a name for himself when he stepped out of the cushy confines of Dutchess County Lanes and went down to nearby Skytop Lanes in Hartsdale, a place made famous by the legendary Ralph Engan. There, he got on the microphone at the front desk one night and challenged everybody in the house. He bowled Engan's protégé, a bowler named Hank Burroughs, and dominated him. News of his destruction of Burroughs quickly spread to the city.

The word on the street was that Blair had a backer named Dobber, another beefy, strapping shylock like Maxie, who funded Blair against all challengers. If he wasn't putting his money down on Blair, he was betting it on a hand of cards or at the horse track—any place where he thought he could leave with more money than he had when he arrived. But the difference between Dobber and Maxie was that Dobber was known to be as cunning with his fists as he was with his money. The streets taught him enough about how to throw a right hand that he became a fighter while honing his craft as a professional gambler. Dobber never sent in any goons; his fists were the goons. And if his fists were not fearsome enough, many believed Dobber packed heat wherever he went. Blair knew that was not true, but he also knew it was best to let those fears fester in his opponents.

Sometimes Dobber took Blair on the short drive from Dutchess County into the five boroughs to see if he could catch some fish with his seventeen-year-old bait. Dobber marched Blair into bowling alleys in the Bronx or Manhattan and asked the locals which of them had the balls to bowl his boy. This was no hustler like Russo or Schlegel; this was a kid who didn't mind letting others learn the hard way that he was better than they were. Blair almost never lost. His accuracy on the lanes was that of a kid that would have tried to fit a spitball through the eye of a needle from a few feet away. The kid never missed his target.

Then Dobber started taking him down to Central. Schlegel and Limongello could not believe their eyes the moment Blair walked in. His presence whipped the place into a buzz about the arrival of the great but largely unseen prodigy, and Schlegel had to have first dibs. If this truly was the best bowler anyone had seen, he would have to beat Schlegel to prove it. Schlegel battled him for several games, one of which culminated in his 300 over Blair's 268. Scores of that magnitude were almost unheard at the time. A bowler who averaged a mere 195 back then was a bowler who rarely lost.

All the "smart money" in the house was on Blair. His reputation was enough to convince the gamblers and shylocks where their money ought to go. But when Blair stepped up to bowl Lemon man-to-man after bowling Schlegel, the contest yielded perhaps the most anticlimactic match in action bowling history. Lemon won the first game 269-268. Then he started the next game with six consecutive strikes. So did Blair. Lemon got up and blasted yet another strike. Blair returned the favor, tossing his seventh straight strike of the game. And that was when the match ended just as soon as it began. Blair's thumb ripped open on that seventh strike, and he had to withdraw from the match. Any number of factors could cause a bowler's thumb to rip open. Sometimes the ball was drilled poorly— maybe the span was too long, or the finger holes were measured improperly. Sometimes the way a bowler released the ball caused the thumb to grate against the thumbhole at the release. Sometimes the skin on a human thumb can only take so many games before it gives way. Whatever the reason, Blair's thumb ripped open that night, and Lemon was furious. There was too much money on the line here, too much of an opportunity to claim the kind of street cred that came with beating a kid who commanded so much respect that every gambler in the joint rushed to put their money down on him.

Lemon never saw the kid again. Blair enlisted in the Navy shortly after graduating high school, leaving a legend in his wake.

While Lemon had Blair to contend with, Schlegel's arch rival in those days was a kid whom he described as the Joe Frazier to his Muhammad Ali. He was also one of the most corrupt shysters to roam Gun Post. His name was Kenny Barber, age 20, better known as "The Rego Park Flash" after his hometown of Rego Park in Queens. Barber's game already had earned him enough of a reputation that writer Jim Kaull produced a feature story about him titled "The Restless One" for the April, 1963 issue of a premier bowling industry magazine called *Bowlers Journal*. Barber's name appeared on the cover. Kaull described Barber as "hanging around street corners, racing around in hot rods and having a good time at society's expense. He never got arrested but he admits that it wasn't because he shouldn't have been." Barber started bowling at age 15. He dropped out of high school by age 16 intent on pursuing a life on the lanes as ardently as he pursued life on the street corner. His father, a great bowler in his own right as well as a traveling musician who played bass and tuba with the likes of Louie Armstrong, Arthur Godfrey, and Tommy Dorsey, had hoped music might be his son's ticket out of the streets and into a life. Barber told Kaull he liked music, too, but "couldn't stick with it."

He spoke with a thick Queens accent and a peculiar lisp that made him sound like he had a mouth half-filled with water. One year, Barber bowled a three-game series of 666 at the American Bowling Congress tournament, one of the most prestigious events in which a bowler could compete. When he got back home, his friends were fond of asking him to tell them what his series was. Barber, who never minded a joke at his own expense, would say "666" with that lisp, and he and his buddies would fall on the floor laughing. That lisp never hampered his skill with the ladies, however. A handsome, bronze-skinned Italian kid with grease-slicked hair and jewel-green eyes, Barber rarely slept with the same woman twice.

Barber was as much a prankster as he was a philanderer. His antics rivaled even those of Iggy Russo. To sabotage opponents, Barber would plant a greased rag on the ball rack. Once they reached for it to wipe the lane oil off their ball, they'd spend the rest of the night trying to figure out why the ball kept slipping off their hands. Barber thought it was hilarious. Another thing he thought was hilarious was "accidentally" slipping and falling on the approach while throwing practice shots before a match. Barber only did it to make his opponent wonder if the approaches were sticky—anything to get the other guy thinking about something other than the task at hand—and worry that they, too, might fall on their asses. Barber, of course, knew the approaches at Gun Post were no more problematic than the approaches anywhere else. He also knew he had his opponents' money in the bag the minute he got them thinking otherwise.

But Barber was equal parts con man and clown. One night he thought it might be a good idea to set off firecrackers inside the bowling alley, so he did, scaring the shit out of everybody there. Most people suspected the culprit was Crazy Vito, a neighborhood gangster for whom Barber collected. Exactly what those collection activities involved, nobody wanted to know. That was the thing about Barber. You never knew which one of his faces was the real Kenny Barber. Maybe the clown was just the mask the con man wore. Maybe the real Barber was the guy who did whatever it took to collect what you owed to Crazy Vito. Nobody knew for sure.

He tempted death as often as he used it to threaten Crazy Vito's debtors.

In an early experience in the action at Brooklyn's Seaview Lanes on Flatlands Avenue in Brooklyn—a desolate part of town known for the fifteen-cent burgers and triple-thick shakes at Farrell's drive-in and for the landfill where mobsters dumped the bodies of those who crossed them—a crew of backers known to put their money on Barber drove him up to the alley to arrange a match. When word got around that a sixteen-year-old Barber would be Mike Chiuchiolo, one of the toughest matches in town, the money handlers started listing bets and taking cash as Barber went to retrieve his ball and bag from the car. He didn't get much farther than fifteen feet from the door before three mobsters stopped to tell him how it was going to be.

"You're gonna lose," one of the gangsters informed Barber, a gun pressed to the back of his head.

The gangsters wanted Barber to dump the match so they could pocket some easy proceeds. They had watched Iggy do it often enough to know it worked, so they did what any good gangster does with a proven idea. They stole it.

Just like some of those horse races and boxing matches guys like Barber loved to bet on, bowling, too, could be fixed. With anything involving money, there always was a way to rob, cheat, or steal. Barber himself was corrupt enough to know that as well as anybody else. On this particular night at Seaview, however, he wasn't letting on.

"I don't know how to lose," he told the gangster.

"You're losing," the gangster repeated.

He pressed the revolver a little tighter against Barber's skull.

"Look," Barber pleaded, "why don't you bet on me? I'm not gonna lose. You can make a lot of money on me!"

"For a sixteen-year-old kid, you sure got a lotta fuck-in' *balls!*" the gangster said in his Brooklyn accent.

Barber matched his flashy looks with some flash on the lanes. He had a unique bowling style in which he would curl up into a ball and then explode at the foul line, and he enjoyed throwing the ball with a big hook that was rare for the era because of the inferior technology in the bowling balls used then. Bowling balls made of hard rubber or plastic, as balls were in the early 1960s, did not possess anywhere near the hook potential of the more technologically advanced equipment that would become available to bowlers in the decades to come. Barber proceeded to thrash Chiuchiolo, beating him nine games straight and making the gangsters who bet on him quite a generous chunk of money. They had his back from that night on.

The youngest player to bowl in the All-Star Tournament in 1963—arguably one of the most prestigious and grueling bowling tournament in the world at the time—a 17-year-old Barber competed alongside legendary names like Don Carter and Dick Weber. He carried a 204 average for 52 games. A month after bowling the All-Star, he shot a nine-game total of 1,940 at the elite American Bowling Congress tournament. He ultimately placed ninth in the "All-Events," which is the combined total a bowler tallies through all three events of the tournament—the singles, doubles, and team events, each of which consists of three games. Before busting his back while running out the final shot of a 299 game one day in a match against Lemon, Barber recorded a high series of 876, shooting scores of 300, 299, and 277 in an action match at Jamaica Arena. Barber averaged 258 for ten games that night.

Barber's triumphs on the lanes did not always culminate in glory. One night, he took some buddies up to a bowling alley in Connecticut looking for action and promptly cleaned the place out to the tune of nearly $10,000. As they headed down the interstate to go back home, somebody cut him off. Then another car came up from behind and shoved him into the shoulder. A few guys got out with guns. Barber and his buddies recognized them as the very bowlers they had just trounced. They had been following Barber's car all along with every intention of getting their money back.

It was exactly the kind of moment when a six-foot-five, 250-pound man known only as "Milo" comes in particularly handy. Luckily for Barber, that is exactly what he happened to have in the passenger seat that night.

"You boys stay here," Milo grunted. "I'll handle this."

Milo got out of the car. He was so huge that when he rose from a seat he never seemed to stop getting up. It was like watching a mountain emerge from the fog. One of the guys pointed his gun at Milo's head. Milo walked up to him and stuck his finger in the barrel.

"We're gonna kill you!" they said.

"You're gonna kill yourself, you stupid bas-tid!" Milo barked. "I've got my finger in the barrel. I'll lose my finger, but you'll lose your life. The gun will backfire and kill you. So now why don't you think about getting the fuck out of here?"

That was enough for the guys with guns to suspect Milo was both insane and eminently serious about trading his finger for their lives. If they had any notion of pondering the plausibility of Milo's take on what happens when you stick your finger in the barrel of a gun, they did not let on. They got back in their car and peeled away.

Nobody pulled any guns when Schlegel and Barber banged heads at a place called Ridgewood Lanes in Brooklyn. Barber knew Schlegel was no scrub from out of town who would abide greased rags and false trips on the approach. He also knew the amount of money that would come down on the match from gamblers and shylocks would be enough to buy the place they bowled in. And Schlegel, for his part, knew Barber was a hell of a bowler who would neither be fooled by a stink of bourbon nor afraid of the gorilla show he put on at Central.

The first time Barber and Schlegel bowled each other, Schlegel shot the first 300 game of his life, beating Barber 300-279. But Schlegel bowled 155 the next game and lost—a development the gamblers would remember next time. It is not always easy for bowlers to come down from the adrenaline rush that accompanies a perfect game. Sometimes a bowler will find himself throwing the ball harder in the next game as his nerves take time to settle down. Any delay in the point at which the ball gets into a roll and finally hooks back toward the pocket—a problem easily caused by throwing the ball too hard—will cause the ball to come up shy of the pocket or even whiff the headpin altogether. The result often can be an ugly, difficult split. As adrenaline caused Schlegel to throw the ball harder than he meant to, those crushing pocket shots he threw against Barber in his 300 game now left splits such as the 5-7 and the 8-10. One fact that makes these tough breaks particularly brutal is that the difference between a strike and a near-pocket shot that leaves an 8-10 split is a matter of centimeters.

The 5 pin is the pin directly behind the headpin, in the second row of pins from the back. The 7 pin is the back-row pin off in the left-hand corner of the pin deck. If a ball comes up "light" rather than hitting the pocket "flush" or dead on, both the 5 and 7 pins might be left simultaneously. The only way to convert such a spare is to kiss the 5 pin across the pin deck and hope it topples over the 7 pin on its way into the left-corner of the pin pit. The 8-10 split, also a consequence of failing to hit the pocket flush, is a considerably more difficult spare. Those pins are both in the back row, leaving less room to finesse the ball just to the left of the 8 pin to send it sailing across the deck into the 10 pin. Additionally, it is easier for a right-handed bowler to nudge the 5 pin off to the left than it is to nudge the 8 pin all the way across the pin deck to the right, just as it is difficult for a left-handed bowler to nudge the 9 pin all the way across the deck to the left to topple over the 7 pin. The harder Schlegel threw his ball in the game following his 300 against Kenny Barber, the more he suffered one open frame after another as he failed to convert the difficult splits he left. Thousands of dollars had exchanged hands by the end of that night, the boisterous collection of gamblers growing more numerous behind the lanes with each passing game. Barber told Schlegel to come back for a rematch a few nights later, easily enough time for word to spread throughout the five boroughs about the big match coming up between Barber and Schlegel.

The place was packed with sharks and gamblers from every corner of New York City by the time they bowled again. Nearly two hundred people were betting on the match behind the lanes. Schlegel won the first game, but then Barber beat him the next three in a row. Schlegel switched bowling balls and shot 299 in game five for $500, and that was when the gamblers remembered what happened the last time Schlegel got that hot. He had shot 155 and lost the next game. There is no loyalty among gamblers; there is only money. So the gamblers cut their bets. All the money now was on Barber, who had upped the ante for the next game to $800. If Schlegel wanted to bowl, he would have to put all the money down out of pocket. It's a lot easier to gamble with somebody else's money than it is to gamble with your own. Bet too much of your own money, and that is when you started to squeeze. Schlegel knew that as well as anyone. But he also knew the only way to make the gamblers wish they had more faith in him was to beat Barber. He started the next game with seven consecutive strikes and won. Then Barber had them move to a new pair of lanes; maybe Schlegel had figured something out that he would lose if they moved. Not so much. Schlegel won the next game, too, and by then all the money in the house—his, Barber's, the gamblers—was where Schlegel liked it best: in his hands.

Schlegel may have won in the end, but those high-profile matches worked miracles for Barber's reputation; he became known as the kind of bowler you wanted to put your money on. He was consistent, whereas Schlegel could run super hot, or very cold. One night at Central, Maxie watched a young lefty out of Connecticut named Larry Lichstein thrash another bowler. Then he watched one of Lichstein's friends walk up to Barber and ask him if he would like to bowl Lichstein.

"How much?" Barber said.

"Two hundred bucks," said Lichstein's friend.

Barber laughed his ass off.

"I don't pick up a ball for less than a grand a game," he said.

Lichstein and his buddy only had a total of $900 on them, just the kind of predicament for which Maxie always kept his crisp roll of hundreds on hand. Maxie had seen enough of Lichstein to know the kid had a hot hand that night. He put up the money and Barber picked up a ball. He soon wished he hadn't. Lichstein beat him the first game for $1,000. Barber asked for double or nothing next game and got it, and Lichstein beat him again for $2,000. Then he did it again for $4,000 the following game. The games were close and Barber kept grinding, but the thing about lefties is that when they get locked in they never miss. And that was the thing about Lichstein on this particular night: He never missed. After Maxie took his cut and Lichstein split the rest with his buddy, Lichstein left the place with $2,000 cash in his pocket. He was a 145-pound, seventeen-year-old kid who knew he had just found the thing he would do for the rest of his life.

Lichstein would prove just as displeased with losing as he was thrilled with winning. One night, having hurt his arm bowling, he decided to make his money betting instead. He put his money on a guy named Vick Pulin, who was bowling Lichstein's fellow Connecticut native, Jim Byrnes. Byrnes was a big, stocky Irishman with forearms the size of boat anchors. Byrnes liked to call Pulin "Stone Fingers." Every time Pulin needed a strike, Byrnes insisted, Pulin's fingers turned to stone; he never had the nerves to come through in the clutch. Byrnes beat Pulin good, and lined his pockets with Lichstein's money.

Lichstein then made it personal. Too personal, he quickly learned.

"Fuck you! When my arm gets better I will *kill* you!" Lichstein screamed at Jim.

"Larry, let's just calm down,'" Byrnes said

"Fuck you!" Lichstein repeated. "You got my money!"

"If you open your mouth one more time, I will pick you up, dump you in the garbage can, and sit on it until you apologize," Byrnes said.

But Lichstein started up again anyway. Byrnes jumped up, picked up Lichstein, and stuffed him into the reeking garbage can.

"Now say another word and I'll break your arm off and stick it up your ass!" Byrnes told him.

Byrnes sat on the lid and did not let Lichstein out for 45 minutes.

Lichstein later would insist that incident was the reason he went bald as an adult.

If bowling was the thing Lichstein wanted to do for the rest of his life, he would not be doing it at Central Lanes. Nobody would. One day Schlegel showed up at Central for more action only to hear the place had been held up the previous night by gangsters armed with machine guns. Such an event was unheard of before then. In these days before credit cards and ATM machines, everybody carried cash. And even though everybody knew that bowling alleys after dark had tens of thousands of dollars in cash getting thrown around on gambling, no one worried about getting robbed. It just did not happen. That it had happened now, and that it happened at one of the most frequented centers of action bowling in the tri-state area, was a grim sign that times were changing.

"You should have been here!" a friend told Schlegel.

"Good thing I wasn't! They would have taken my money," Schlegel said.

Had they taken his life, well, that would have been bad, too. But not as bad as it would have been had they taken his money, he figured. But more importantly, where would the action go now that Central Lanes was gone?

The specter of an armed robbery at Central sent the action scurrying for another new home. But even if the action kept coming to Central after that, it would not have come for long. The owner died, and within months, the place burned to the ground. Some believed the owner's daughters had it torched for the insurance money; others maintained it was an accident resulting from a couple of kids screwing around with fire in a utility closet. But it didn't matter now. Central was gone for good by 1967, and its demise also marked the demise of action bowling's golden era. Several years had passed since the early days at Avenue M Bowl. Some of those baby-faced kids who bet on Mac and Stoop back then were not such kids anymore. They shaved. They had moved out of their parents' house. They had steady girlfriends pestering them about marriage, kids, and the kinds of jobs normal people kept. Others got drafted and, when they returned, jobs. By then, the now-real threat of robbery or dumpers like Russo who fomented distrust also had taken their toll on the action bowling scene.

Of all the factors that contributed to this decline in action bowling, one of the biggest was that the scene's marquee stars pulled out to pursue even greener pastures. Barber went into the pro shop business and soon developed an empire of shops throughout the New York metropolitan area. His acumen as an entertainer gifted him with people skills others go to school to learn, and that big personality proved to be a goldmine in business. You did not just go to Kenny Barber to get a new bowling ball drilled up; you went to Kenny Barber for a show. Whether he was drilling your ball or giving you video lessons and film feedback out on the lanes—an idea he conceived years before it became vogue to do so—Barber was just as likely to deliver a gut-splittingly funny stand-up comedy act as he was to show you where to stand on a given lane condition or measure your span for a new ball.

Johnny Petraglia and Mike McGrath went on to bowl the Professional Bowlers Association tour. Lichstein later followed them there and became Rookie of the Year in 1969 before taking up a gig as Player Services Director. Like many others who had lived and breathed action bowling every day of their lives for years, Steve Harris succumbed to a nagging feeling that it was time to grow up; he left his pro shop behind for a gig on Wall Street. Others, too, vanished into lives far removed from bowling, backers, and big bets. As the scene gradually lost its big names and big gamblers, it also lost its identity. Even after Harris moved on with his life, he would, on occasion, head out to one of the bowling alleys he once frequented only to find it desolate at a time of night when it once was frenzied with gamblers and the bowlers they bet on. He would ask around about where the action had gone. Some had no answer for him; others sent him to places they swore the action still could be found, and Harris would go to again find nobody there. Times had changed; that world was gone.

For Ernie Schlegel, the greatest action bowler New York City had ever seen, there was no Plan B. There was only bowling. But Schlegel's road to the PBA Tour would be far more treacherous than the one that guys like Petraglia, McGrath, and Lichstein took. There would be knife fights and long nights, dragnets and gang wars, hard luck and hope. Most of all, there would be an enduring suspicion that nothing comes easily when you are Ernie Schlegel.

4

THE ROAD TO BUFFALO

S chlegel knew his road to the PBA would be a tough one
long before Central Lanes burned to the ground. He knew
it the night he buried a blade in a buddy's chest amid an
argument over twenty bucks.

The fight began with a suggestion heard frequently at Schlegel's haunt on Broadway and Sherman Avenue in Inwood, a
bowling alley called Manhattan Lanes: "Go fuck yourself."
It was a place owned by a businessman named Emil Lence,
who owned several bowling centers throughout the country.
On Mondays, Schlegel watched Lence stroll through the place
with a cigar in his face, a fedora, a long coat, and a bodyguard
the size of a Buick on either side of him to haul his business's
cash into a truck out in the street. Just the place, then, for the
kind of salty language directed at Schlegel on this particular
afternoon. The person directing that language his way was a
portly, Jewish kid named Mike Ginsberg who happened to be a

commendable action bowler himself. Ginsberg owed Schlegel money, and he did not take too kindly to Schlegel's request that $20 of it be paid on the spot one afternoon. As Ginsberg would learn, most people who told Schlegel to go fuck himself did so only once.

A lot of people in Schlegel's life found themselves in that particular company by then. It was 1962; Schlegel, now age 19, soon would be moving out of his parents' place on Sickles Street and shacking up with a couple buddies in a three-bed-room apartment for a grand total of $150 a month. One of Schlegel's roommates was Jerry Markey, who first saw Schlegel while attending a Boy Scouts meeting with his friend Mike McKeean one Friday night. Markey looked out the window at one point and saw Schlegel, dead-drunk and staggering with a zip gun in his hand. A kid had broken Schlegel's nose in a street brawl, so Schlegel told him he was going to get his gun and come back to shoot him in the face. He promptly did exactly as he had promised. He went home, assembled and loaded his zip gun, and then went back out and found the kid. A riotous commotion ensued in which Schlegel was separated from his zip gun, likely saving his intended target's life.

"Who the hell is that guy?" Markey asked McKeean.

"Oh, that's Ernie Schlegel," McKeean said.

The way McKeean said Schlegel's name sounded as much like a forewarning as it sounded like an answer to Markey's question.

Schlegel had learned much from Ginsberg over the years. He watched how Ginsberg worked back at Gun Post, the way he used his wiseass mouth to cajole players like Tony the Milkman or Mike the Cab Driver into bowling him for more money than they could afford to wager. How he would give guys so much shit that they would keep betting more money out of anger. When Ginsberg finally got his opponents to bet with their emotions rather than their minds, he knew he had them beaten. Schlegel watched Ginsberg pay his own way through college this way. It was Ginsberg whom Schlegel credited for turning him into the chest-pounding gorilla of Central Lanes, Ginsberg who showed him how to bleed money from the driest stone.

Ginsberg tutored Schlegel in the discipline practiced by the greatest gamblers. Schlegel watched Ginsberg's opponents try to turn the tables on him, hoping to lure him into a match he didn't care to bowl, nudge him out of his comfort zone. They called him an arrogant Jew. They called him a fat Jew bastard. Anything they could think of to get him to lace up his shoes and put some money down. Nothing worked. No one could embarrass or enrage him enough to get him on the lanes. That was the steel exterior of a guy who had his shit together, and Schlegel knew it.

"You never get on the lanes until you got an edge," Ginsberg would tell Schlegel. "If you think you're better, you can win."

The smart action bowlers never allowed emotion to interfere with their judgment. The sooner a player got you emotional enough to bowl, the sooner he stuffed his pockets with your rent money. But one thing Schlegel would also come to understand was that at Manhattan Lanes, to ask for money upfront from a guy who owed it to you was to ask for the fight of your life. Eight weeks had passed since Schlegel lent Ginsberg $155, and Ginsberg had yet to pay back a dime. So one afternoon while Schlegel kicked back some brews at the bowling alley bar, he happened to spot Ginsberg. Schlegel asked him for twenty bucks and reminded him of his debt.

"Go fuck yourself. I ain't paying you back shit," Ginsberg said.

"Fuck you!" Schlegel said. "Man, if I had you outside!"

"Yeah? Well fuck you! Let's go!" Ginsberg said.

Such were the means of conflict resolution practiced in the bowling alleys of New York City in 1962. This particular conflict, however, would take quite a bit more to resolve than the usual opprobrium of the street.

Now Ginsberg, too, was about to meet the Other Ernie.

Ginsberg hurled Schlegel through a plate-glass window and out into the street. Schlegel, dusted in a coating of shattered glass, got up off the ground.

"Fuck you! I'll kill you!" Schlegel said.

But Ginsberg kept coming at him. He swung once at Schlegel and missed. Then Schlegel reached for the blade he kept in his pocket. He buried it in Ginsberg's chest. Yet Ginsberg, as much of a stocky bull off the lanes just as he was on the lanes, kept coming at him still. He smashed Schlegel once more. Schlegel hit him with a left. Finally, Ginsberg slipped bloodily down the hood of a parked cab. A friend grabbed the knife and ran. Schlegel never saw that knife again.

Schlegel rose from the blood and shattered glass, his torn jeans revealing two scraped and bleeding knees. Then he did what any reasonable person might do after stabbing somebody: He went home, cleaned himself up, and went back to the Manhattan Lanes bar.

Which was exactly where the cops hoped to find him—and did.

"Are you Ernie Schlegel?" they asked.

Schlegel returned the question with one of his own, a not particularly wise strategy under the scrutiny of New York City cops who suspect you just tried to kill somebody.

"Who wants to know?" Schlegel said.

"*We* do!"

Clearly, the cops would be the only ones asking questions.

The cops dragged Schlegel out of the bar and delivered him to Jewish Memorial Hospital on Broadway at 196th Street. There, they brought him into Ginsberg's room.

"He stabbed me!" Ginsberg said, pointing at Schlegel from his bed.

The cops looked at Schlegel. Schlegel shrugged.

"I didn't stab nobody," Schlegel said. "We got in a fight. What are you gonna do?"

A skilled defense attorney, Ernie Schlegel was not.

"He stabbed me," Ginsberg repeated.

The cops believed him. They booked Schlegel into the 34th precinct, badgering him until, they hoped, they might wear him down.

"Where's the knife?" they would ask him.

"What knife?" Schlegel would answer.

This went on for hours. The cops charged him with attempted murder and sent him to a cell where he stayed the night. He lit his pack of smokes down to the last cigarette, one after the other, until he was left with only four unused matches. He peeled those in half and smoked them, too, as he tried to keep his mind off the swollen and throbbing hand he had crashed into Ginsberg's skull.

"Never get arrested on a Friday night," Schlegel thought to himself. "Especially when you have only four smokes and four matches left."

Schlegel's mother, Irma, who came to America from Nazi Germany just as Hitler was rising to power, proved especially unimpressed with the aftermath of her son's blow-out with Ginsberg. Schlegel never knew if the story was true, but he had heard that his mother once spit at Hitler. She found him holed up in a jail cell with a right hand bloated to the size of a mango, a black eye from a cop's cocked fist, and his bloodied face emblazoned with the pattern of the corduroy coat he had slept on. The shaggy, blonde hair that had earned him the nickname "Strawhead" looked like the nest of some livid crow.

"What did you do to my son?" Schlegel's mother screamed in her thick German accent.

This didn't look to her like something that happened in America. It looked more like something that happened in the country she left behind.

A doctor told a grand jury soon thereafter that it looked to him as though Ginsberg had been stabbed. It looked, in fact, as though Ginsberg was lucky to be alive. The knife went in right under Ginsberg's heart, leaving a clean wound doctors sutured with a couple of butterfly stiches.

Things did not look good for Schlegel, but the streets of Inwood had a way of cultivating experts in the field of "things that don't look good." That expertise was about to spare Schlegel from calling the clink home for years to come. Luck may have guarded Ginsberg's heart from the jab of Schlegel's knife, but it would prove utterly powerless against the war of attrition that followed. Schlegel found his soldiers among the many other people who owed him a buck. They now had the chance to dissolve their debt with little more than a few well-chosen words on the witness stand. Everybody who owed Schlegel money, it seemed, found their way to the courthouse to pay their debts more handsomely than cash alone ever could. Each of them testified before the grand jury as to the quality of Schlegel's character. By the time they were done, they had turned Schlegel into a man whose character was as unimpeachable as the Pope's. The grand jury, however, proved rather less than convinced.

If Schlegel knew anything at this moment in his life, it was this: He was not going to jail. Few people could turn a crisis into a fortune like Ernie Schlegel. From adolescence, he could pick up the scent of a dollar as quickly as a wolf picks up the smell of blood in the woods. At age fourteen, he found the scent in nearby homes where he earned pocket money cleaning ovens and windows for housewives. He found it in the window he broke through with friends to steal ice cream and hot dogs at a restaurant in Fort Tryon Park. He found it in the 7Up factory where he spent summers working from 7 A.M. to midnight, and he found it in the bowling alleys where he spent what was left of his sleepless nights hustling con men and clowns. He only slept by accident in those days, and that was fine by him. By the time he was holding down that gig with 7Up, he worked so much that he never had time to spend what he made. If the money he made there still was not enough to satisfy him, then there were the televisions his friends would steal and deliver to him for $200, which Schlegel quickly turned around on the street for $225. Or the '48 Jaguar he bought for $30 and sold days later for $75.

It was no different in 1962. He sold everything he owned, saved everything he earned, and soon had what he needed— enough money to make a lawyer care what happened to him. Schlegel's girlfriend at the time knew a guy named Mr. Richardson, who knew a lawyer. Schlegel stuffed a suitcase with every dollar he had scrounged and went to see the lawyer in his office. He pushed his money across the lawyer's desk and explained what had happened in the street outside Manhattan Lanes that day.

"I can't go to jail," he said.

The lawyer took the money and proceeded to request more time from the judge every time he went to court on Schlegel's behalf. And so began Schlegel's war of attrition against Mike Ginsberg, who kept taking days off from his job with Jonathan Logan, a wildly popular brand of dresses in the 1960s, to attend court hearings only to discover that they had been postponed. Finally, after so many postponements that Ginsberg did not bother showing up anymore, the charges were dismissed. Neither the cops nor the prosecutor could turn up enough evidence to prove definitively that Schlegel had, in fact, stabbed Ginsberg. The only hard evidence Ginsberg himself could provide were the few butterfly stitches it took to heal the wound.

But the fundamental problem had not been dismissed. If anything, his triumph over Mike Ginsberg proved a pyrrhic victory at best. The charges may have been dismissed on paper, but they lingered in the minds of the men who guarded the gates of the PBA. A bowler needed signatures from three sponsors as well as the approval of a PBA executive before he could compete on the PBA Tour. Schlegel soon learned there was something about kids with attempted murder charges in their pasts that made it tough for potential sponsors to find their pens. Nobody wanted to sponsor him. Then Schlegel dug himself a deeper hole while at a bowling alley called Paramus Lanes in Paramus, New Jersey. Frank Esposito, a founding member of the PBA, opened the place in 1955. His contacts in the TV business played a big role in helping the PBA secure its contract with ABC, the network that broadcast the championship round of PBA tournaments each week. He eventually expanded Paramus Lanes into a 42-lane establishment that attracted the greatest stars in the sport. It also was one of those places Schlegel referred to as his "office," a place where the action was as big as the names it attracted, and the money flowed for those who had what it took to take it home. Schlegel was one of those who had what it took.

One night Esposito took exception to the kind of crowd Schlegel brought with him, an unruly posse of hangers-on who talked like sailors and let the ashes of their Lucky Strikes smudge Esposito's new carpet. They might as well have soiled the man's living room rug. Schlegel was not there to babysit his buddies; he was there to make money. Esposito knew how to keep out the riff-raff: Kick out the guy they followed in. He told Schlegel to get the hell out and not come back. That was a lot like sacking Schlegel from his job, as it meant he no longer could count on the money he made there fleecing lesser players of their lunch money in the middle of the night.

The implications of Schlegel's run-in with Esposito extended much further than that. Esposito's dual role as owner of one of the most famous bowling alleys in the northeast and an executive board member with the PBA meant Schlegel had little chance of going pro so long as Esposito had anything to say about it. Esposito had heard enough about Schlegel—the knife he buried in Ginsberg's chest, the zip guns he wielded outside Boy Scouts meetings. And he had finally had enough that night at Paramus. The PBA was a place for groomed men with pressed slacks, parted hair, and wooden smiles; it was not, Esposito thought, a place for Ernie Schlegel. So Schlegel watched helplessly as buddies like Petraglia, Limongello, and Lichstein bowled for real money on national television. Schlegel did not understand how it was possible that one man, Frank Esposito, could wield so much authority as to single-handedly deny him his dreams. To deny him his dreams also was to deny him his livelihood, as his reputation as a great action bowler was making it harder than ever to find an opponent willing to put money down on a match against him on a rapidly shrinking underground scene. He needed the pro tour because he needed to live. Schlegel was the king of the action, and any gambler with half a mind knew it was a lot cheaper to let him be king than it was to try to steal his crown.

One afternoon Steve Harris phoned with news of action bowlers in Jersey who knew so little about this reluctant king that they would put up money to bowl him. Harris, at this time in his life, was earning an advanced degree in the art of bullshitting that served him well in the action. He was working customer service for the Baumritter Corporation, the company that later became Ethan Allen. Harris was taking complaints from customers by phone and repeating them into a Dictaphone, which he then delivered to a pool of typists to transcribe. Company policy mandated that Harris work under a phony name. His name at Baumritter was James Warren. The pseudonym used by his neighboring colleague, an African-American woman named Judy Brown, was Douglas Reed.

"What's wrong with Steve Harris?" Harris would complain to his bosses. "Why do I need a phony name?"

"Steve Harris will leave someday," they told him. "James Warren will be here forever."

One day Harris took a call from a guy in Mississippi with a thick, southern drawl asking for "Douglas Reed." Harris played the part.

"This is Douglas Reed," he said.

"Hi, Doug! How are you?" the exuberant southerner drawled.

"I'm fine, sir. How are you?" Harris said.

"Doug, I got a question for you," the man said. "I hear that Baumritter Corporation is full of niggers and Jews."

"Fuck you!" Harris shouted, and then hung up the phone with an angry bang.

Harris was petrified; Judy Brown nearly fainted. He explained the reason he hung up on the guy.

"Good!" she said. Harris's feisty personality was beginning to shine through.

Harris spent his working hours making deals with disgruntled customers, offering them discounts and other perks to keep them off his manager's case. He thought he had spotted a deal of his own the night he called Schlegel with news Schlegel had received from Harris before.

"Ernie, we got fish in Jersey," Harris said when his friend answered the phone.

Schlegel hardly made it past "Hello" before he and his crew were halfway up the Major Deegan Expressway, looking for an easy score. The fish Harris found this time were a group of Jersey milkmen who would bowl for money after their runs at about 5 A.M. on Sundays. Nagai was tied up with business at his restaurant that night, so they called up One Finger Benny, the man who could bowl 180 using just one finger. He would find gamblers willing to spot him thirty or forty pins, sure they were good enough to beat him anyway if he was going to bowl with just one finger. Benny won almost every time. It was as lucrative a gag as anything Iggy Russo ever pulled off. But Benny also had a car. He called his friend Sammy Mauro, an ex-con and an excellent bowler whose soft-spoken manner belied his brawny frame and chiseled arms. Together they picked up Harris and Schlegel and headed down to Jersey.

By the end of the night, a penniless Schlegel found himself on the side of a freeway, walking home with his bowling bag at his side and yet another reluctant title to add to his reputation: accomplice. Those milkmen they met down in Jersey proved at least as proficient at bowling as they were at leaving milk bottles on doorsteps. They wiped out Schlegel and his crew. With less than $10 between them, they got into Benny's car and headed back over the George Washington Bridge. Then Sammy got an idea.

"Take Ogden Avenue," he told Benny. "A guy there owes me money."

It was about 7 A.M. by then. Harris and Schlegel were half asleep in the back seat. Benny pulled up to an Ogden Avenue deli. Sammy got out. Moments later, he stormed back into the car and screamed, "Hit it!"

Benny peeled out and said, "How much did you get?"

"One hundred and sixty dollars," Sammy said.

Benny headed back for the Major Deegan.

"Ernie, we got one hundred and sixty bucks to play with!"
Harris woke up.

"Did you just hold up that place?" he asked.

"What do you care?" Benny said.

"Ernie, these guys just held up a deli," Harris said.

Harris saw mug shots and prison pajamas in his immediate future. He told Benny to stop the car and let them out right there and then. They did, and Harris and Schlegel—who was still nervous from his near miss with the Ginsberg stabbing—walked home together in the blue-black dawn, broke and desperate for a bed to help them forget the night. The farther Schlegel travelled in pursuit of an anonymity he no longer enjoyed in the five boroughs, the more his life reminded him that it was time to move on. Schlegel was getting older; he was watching friends find glory on tour just as he struggled just to find willing challengers in a fading action bowling scene; and he was certain that the life of a bum awaited him, a long nightmare of squandered talent, thwarted ambition, and dead-end jobs.

———•———

If Schlegel had any notion of pursuing a career in bowling, he would have to flee the underworld of action for the legitimacy of the pro tour. But thanks to Esposito, that would not be happening anytime soon. Bowling, the one skill Schlegel had mastered so thoroughly as to squeeze some kind of living out of it, teased him with dreams he once took for granted. He had no money now after giving it all up to cleanse his record of attempted murder charges. He was smoking dope and dealing it. He no longer saw any future in bowling, and that hurt most of all. It hurt watching buddies bowl on national

TV while he was kept off the tour by bad breaks, bitter men, and his own temper/impulsive decisions. Schlegel descended into the driftless life of a dope dealer hawking stolen TVs and old Jaguars. He dumped his bowling ball and bowling shoes off the George Washington Bridge; maybe if he didn't have to look at them anymore, it would be easier to smudge out the hurt in his heart.

Only the streets would welcome him now—streets whose story Schlegel knew too well. In the late 1950s, when Schlegel was in his mid-teens, they were streets where gangs like the Hearts, the Vigilantes, and the Alleycats convened around their territory's candy stores with leather coats and thick hair greased into a duck's ass. Schlegel ran with gangs of German and Irish friends from around the block. They ran down Bennett Avenue armed with clubs and knives. They ran from maniacs in rival gangs who chased them out of Fort Tryon Park with axes. They ran through yards and alleyways and jumped fences to evade dragnets. Sometimes they ran from their own mistakes.

But that was then. Now, as America entered its post-Kennedy delirium in Vietnam, the ducktails and gang wars gave way to the spectacle of kids coming back from the war hooked on heroin. One of Schlegel's best friends, a local kid known as "Tiny," died on the roof of his Sickles Street apartment building. Tiny had been shooting up with some friends when a few of them came banging on Schlegel's door.

"What the hell are you doing?" Schlegel shouted when he opened his door.

"Tiny's OD'ing! Tiny's OD'ing!" they screamed.

They told Schlegel to get some salt. They wanted to shoot salt water in his veins, thinking it would dilute the drugs in Tiny's body and save him. Somehow, they succeeded in bringing the kid back to life, but he died two weeks later. The New York City

Schlegel knew in the mid-1960s was a place where the madness of the times claimed many other friends who were just as acquainted with the forces that drove Tiny to his death—the needle, the bottle, the war—and how easily those forces withstood injections of saline on the rooftops of Inwood. One was killed in Vietnam. Another survived Vietnam only to die drunk in a car accident soon after coming home. One drank himself to death at twenty-five and was found in a Harlem alley. Two others overdosed on heroin. Still another was sent to jail for heroin and came out crippled.

You knew a lot of things as a kid on the streets of Inwood back then, and not all of them had to do with drugs. You knew to stay away from the food at Al's Candy Store, where "Dirty Al's" oily hair had a habit of finding its way into your bacon and egg sandwich. You knew to stay away from Father Martin, whose altar boys were as likely to cross themselves as they were to get a hand down their pants. You knew to stay clear of Clancy the Cop, a sadist who fell in love with the sound his stick made when it cracked the skulls of kids in his precinct.

Another thing Schlegel knew back then was that he had friends who would not let him give up the dream he surrendered after his misadventures with Ginsberg and Esposito. One friend in particular, an action bowler named Pete Mylenki, showed up at the door of Schlegel's apartment one night. The place looked like a bomb had hit it. Schlegel himself looked like a guy who lived in a taxi. He had not shaved in weeks, his clothes were disheveled and soiled, and he kept his strawberry-blond hair long and wild.

Schlegel had won a lot of money with Mylenki. Mylenki was such a clutch action bowler that Schlegel often found himself picking up the money from the score table anytime Mylenki needed to strike in the 10th frame for the win, so certain was he that Mylenki would come through. He always did. Unlike most other action bowlers, Mylenki was a clean-cut kid who showed up to bowl in a white, button-down shirt and big, black, horn-rimmed glasses. Most of the other action players showed up in jeans and T-shirts. They looked the part; Mylenki didn't. Schlegel picked him up as a doubles partner because no one knew who he was, and a kid who dressed like that in the action looked an awful lot like a fish to the scene's usual suspects. Until he started bowling.

The Pete Mylenki who showed up at Schlegel's apartment a few years later wasn't looking for a doubles partner. He was looking to pay back a friend in a currency far more lasting than money—the currency of friendship. Mylenki locked eyes with Schlegel through a vaguely blue and chalky haze of weed that thickened the air inside the place and altered the direction of Schlegel's life forever. He looked over the devastation of the apartment and shook his head.

"Ernie, this ain't you. You gotta straighten out," Mylenki told him. "I got a job for you in Jersey. I got you a place to live out there, too. You start Monday."

Mylenki had landed Schlegel a job cleaning air-conditioning units out in Hackensack.

"I don't even have a car," Schlegel told him.

"You can find one when you get there," Mylenki said before leaving.

Mylenki may not quite have understood at the time that the haze of hydro hanging over the obliterated and rollicking apartment he entered that night was as much a part of Schlegel as the fabled "Other Ernie." As with that latter, morbidly violent half of him, the Schlegel that Mylenki found in that Inwood shanty also needed to be saved from himself. Mylenki's connection with an air-conditioning technician in Hackensack who happened to want an assistant was all he needed to make that happen. Naturally, Schlegel and his friends found a way to turn Mylenki's miraculous intervention into another occasion for sordid debauchery.

"Guys!" Schlegel shouted as he turned to his friends upon Mylenki's departure, "I got a job starting Monday! Toga party!"

It was the last weekend that Schlegel would live with his roommates, Dicky Bott and Jerry Markey, the final party he and his friends would host in that apartment, and the last time many of them would see each other for fifty years. But they made sure, on their way out, that the landlord would never forget who lived there. He came banging on the door to yell at them about the noise. Markey opened the door and said "We're leaving Monday!" Then he slammed the door in the landlord's face, and the party went on. The apartment quaked with the Isley Brothers' "Shout" on full blast; Schlegel and the boys flipped up the volume fast every time they heard the word "Shout" and screamed it together.

Schlegel moved to Westwood, New Jersey and bought a beat-up station wagon for $125. He would spray the air conditioning units of Hackensack looking for air bubbles that betrayed the spot at which Freon leaked out. Their boss also had an account at one of the YMCA's in New York City. There, Schlegel and Chuck installed air-conditioning units in the windows in May and removed them come October. He did this work for several years.

Thanks to this period on the straight and narrow for the first time since elementary school, Schlegel returned to bowling. Mylenki would not leave him alone until he did. He saw the dream in Schlegel's eyes, however much Schlegel himself tried to turn away from it.

"You have to follow your dream, Ernie," Mylenki told Schlegel.

"I tried everything," Schlegel said. "I can't."

"Yes, you can," Mylenki said. "You have to. This is not the way you want to live the rest of your life. You weren't born to fix air-conditioning units. You were born to bowl."

When Schlegel looked in the mirror, he saw a broken-down young man with nowhere to go. Mylenki saw someone else; he saw a dreamer who still had a shot. By 1967, he was essentially running Schlegel's life. He placed Schlegel in several bowling leagues. Schlegel would put in a day's work in Hackensack and then, two or three nights a week, he would head off to bowl a few games of league. He started getting a taste of what he had left behind. He started feeling the itch he hadn't scratched in years—the itch of the gambler, the itch of that chest-pounding gorilla who lorded over Central Lanes years ago, the itch of a guy who just wanted to be somebody.

Then Mylenki got in Esposito's ear. He wanted Schlegel to bowl an upcoming PBA Tour event. Toru Nagai, Schlegel's old cohort from his very first days in the action, agreed to sponsor him.

"Well, can you can you clean him up a little?" Esposito asked Mylenki.

"Oh, Frank, come on," Mylenki said.

"No, I *mean* it. Clean him up and we'll let him bowl—otherwise, no."

Mylenki must have gotten Schlegel looking clean enough for Esposito's taste, because Schlegel bowled a PBA regional event in Newburgh, New York, soon thereafter. The regionals are the minor leagues of the PBA, local tournaments for less money where the area's aspiring pros lock horns on the lanes. Those who dominated their regions would be ready for a taste of the national PBA Tour. Some had success there. Others—most others—learned it was time to find a day job.

To Esposito's chagrin, Schlegel led the tournament first game to last and walked away with the top prize. Mylenki pushed Esposito a little harder, leveraging Schlegel's victory. Esposito let him bowl again—this time, a national stop, the 1967 PBA Camden Open in Camden, New Jersey, in late November. Schlegel led the first round, then finished in 9th place in a field dotted with future Hall of Famers. One of those future Hall of Famers—Mike Limongello—finished ten places behind Schlegel, at 19th.

There was no way Esposito could justify his opposition to Schlegel's desire to become a PBA member now. That knife fight with Ginsberg was a distant memory as the calendar turned to 1968. And as for those kids who smudged Esposito's carpet with the smokes at Paramus Lanes, Schlegel had not seen any of them in years. He was holding down an honest job in Hackensack. Esposito finally agreed to let Schlegel become a PBA member.

In the winter of 1969, at the Greater Buffalo Open, Schlegel finally broke through. He qualified as the fourth seed to bowl the nationally televised championship round on ABC. He had survived 42 games of competition against the greatest bowlers on the planet. After eighteen games he was in the top five. He maintained his position for most of the tournament, but it was close. His middle finger was sore, so he kept opening the finger hole with a bevel until it was large enough to keep the pressure off. It worked, and now, finally, here was the future he had been waiting for.

But this was Ernie Schlegel, so there had to be something more to overcome, some additional adversity that would give him the chance to prove to himself that his dreams could only deny him as long as he allowed them to. No one was burying knives in anyone's chest this time; no one was tossing his dreams off the George Washington Bridge. No, this time—for once—the obstacle Schlegel faced was not named Ernie Schlegel. Rather, its name was Mother Nature, and she was sporting her full winter regalia as Buffalo found itself in the throes of a blinding blizzard. In March, no less.

"Why would anybody live here?" Schlegel thought as he toppled an Everest of snow off the windshield of his car. Man-sized snow drifts flanked the roads. Schlegel dug the driver-side door out of the snow it was caked in, pulled the door free of the ice that had frozen shut the lock, and headed to the bowling alley.

Schlegel could not sleep the night before. So he borrowed a page from the days of toga parties and the Isley Brothers: He rolled himself a fatty and fell asleep sitting up in bed.

The trouble Schlegel faced at Fair Lanes in Buffalo the following day was that in any given week on tour, Schlegel faced hundreds of other Ernie Schlegels, men who also grew up in the tough terrain of bowling alleys and proved that they were the best bowlers anyone in town had ever seen. They, too, had dangled by their fingernails from the cliffs of their egos and clawed back to the top often enough to believe that nothing could bring them down. Every bowler on tour believed that, but most of them had headed out of town for the next tour stop by show time that week in Buffalo—most, that is, except for the five bowlers slated to compete before a national audience on ABC.

The kind of pressure that a twenty-five-year-old Ernie Schlegel faced under the steaming lights of TV cameras that snowy afternoon was not the kind relieved by a mere loosening of the finger holes in his bowling ball. Busting the budgets of Jersey kids at Paramus Lanes on Friday nights was one thing five years ago, but trying to do it against the greatest bowlers in the world with the nation looking on was quite another. With only a handful of channels available to viewers in 1969, nearly ten million people carved time out of their Saturdays to make room for the pro bowling telecast on ABC. That was quite a stage for the first-generation American son of a superintendent to leap onto for the first time in his life.

The Ernie Schlegel that announcers Keith Jackson and Billy Welu introduced to the nation at the start of the show had the pensive countenance of a president reading a Soviet telegram threatening nuclear holocaust. They introduced the five contestants one at a time; each got up and threw one shot as his name was announced to the applauding crowd. Schlegel was the only one of the five to whirl through his one shot about as quickly as a bullet blows through a cake. He was already halfway through his hurried approach to the foul line when his name was called, and unlike the other four contenders, he hardly paused to watch his ball strike the pins before darting back to his seat at the pace of a jogger getting chased by a slobbering Doberman.

Schlegel's polo shirt was buttoned to the chin. His hair was greased to the consistency of glass and parted cleanly off to the right—a rigidity that belied the storming spirit inside him. For now, he was merely the kid from Sickles Street in New York City who, as Billy Welu said in his introduction, was "completing his first full year on the tour."

Welu's partner in the booth was Keith Jackson. Jackson's beady eyes were pinched into his round, doughy face. His dark tie was flawlessly knotted in the center of a collar so tight that the flesh of his neck looked like a pot of steaming milk about to boil over.

"If it sounds like I'm carrying the rigors of winter on my back, you're right, I am," he said to apologize for his haggard voice.

It was 1969, after all; you could still say things like that and expect to be taken seriously. Jackson would cover sports for ABC for the next thirty-seven years. His voice would become synonymous with college football, and he would rank among America's most beloved sportscasters. Here in the snows of Buffalo in 1969, that was all decades away, and there was a pro bowling show to get on with. The crowd was decked with horn-rimmed glasses, beehive hairdos, women sporting the wool dresses that Jackie Kennedy made famous, and men lighting cigarettes as casually as kids watching the afternoon pass by from a buddy's stoop. Nearly every man wore a suit and tie and was freshly shaven. These were men who were not too far removed from the days when no man left the house without his fedora.

Everyone's eyes turned toward the pair of lanes where the afternoon's matches were about to unfold. Steve Wallace, the fortunate son of wealthy parents out of Houston—and Ernie Schlegel's opponent—stepped up to throw the first shot of the game. A nineteen-year-old psychology major out of the University of Houston who dropped out to try his luck on tour, Wallace's wiry frame prompted Welu to joke that Wallace weighed "one hundred twenty-five pounds soaking wet, with bowling ball," during his introduction. His clothes hung from his body like a shirt left out on a laundry wire in the wind. He looked as if he were nothing more than a cadaver dressed in a young man's shirt and pants—bowling's own Ichabod Crane. His jet-black pair of Buddy Holly glasses contrasted so sharply against his snow-white complexion that he looked like he had the eyes of a raccoon. Even at the tender age of nineteen, a receding hairline broadened his forehead.

Wallace's opening shot was a bad one. He spared, took his seat, and left the lanes to Schlegel. Schlegel now prepared to throw his first shot on national television. He hid his wild-ness well with manners so staid as to be supine—just the way Esposito and the boys wanted it—despite the $6,000 top prize. But the one place where he could not conceal the wild man within him was his eyes, which narrowed into a reptilian squint as he stared down his target on the lane. He looked like a lizard closing in on a fly.

Schlegel lost the war with his nerves and left a split. He sauntered back to the ball return, then turned toward the split he left as if checking to see if that really just happened. Seeing that in fact it had, he frowned with a mixture of embarrassment and disgust. Here he was with the jewel of his dreams more within reach than ever before, and he was blowing it right out of the gate.

Wallace hurried through two more poor shots and converted his spares as Jackson noted a suspicion that "at nineteen years of age he feels the pressure perhaps a little bit more than some of the veterans." Perhaps. Or maybe Wallace didn't get his degree in the game of survival from the same school that Schlegel attended as a kid—the school where you won the match you were betting on or you couldn't pay the rent tomorrow, where a quarrel over twenty bucks was enough to get you a knife through the chest. Maybe those were the lessons Schlegel applied when he stepped up for his third shot of the match and sent the pins scattering across the deck as if they were just a fistful of dice.

He demolished the pocket yet again on his next shot, but this time left the right-hander's nemesis: the ten pin off in the corner, which is famous for withstanding the best shot a bowler can throw. He winced as he returned to wait for his ball to come back. One game of bowling offered ten chances to end up with a better score than the other guy. To blow one of them on a perfect shot was to tempt fate once too often. But Schlegel gathered himself and made the spare.

And with that the telecast broke for a trip through the commercial wilderness of late 1960s America. There, the brand new 1969 Lincoln Mercury Cyclone was loaded with a 428ci V8, STP

Motor Oil was stronger even than Rocky Marciano, and the BIC pen took another savage pounding and "writes first time, every time." You could get one for just 19 cents—unless you wanted the BIC fine point. That would set you back an entire quarter.

The $6,000 check that had the winner's name on it at the end of the PBA Greater Buffalo Open show was enough to buy two of those Lincoln Mercury Cyclones, enough to keep a man on tour for years to come. It was just a couple grand less than the average median income in 1969, in fact, and enough to put 50 percent down on the total cost of the average house. No one knew what motive flashed through Steve Wallace's mind when he came out of the commercial break to treat the crowd to the two finest shots they had seen all afternoon, blowing the pins straight back into the pit as if struck by a Tom Seaver fast ball. Maybe he had his eye on that Cyclone; maybe he planned to blow pins back into the pit on tour for as long as he could. Or maybe six-thousand bucks was no motive at all to a nineteen-year-old whose parents had the dough to bankroll any dream he had. Perhaps that was the reason for the observation Jackson shared about just how at ease Wallace seemed before the cameras rolled that afternoon.

"Harry Smith, our statistician, noted before we went on the air that young Wallace appeared very loose," Jackson said. "He was a little tight the first couple of frames, but he seems to be loosening up."

The men Schlegel faced in all those nights of hustling back home may not have been any better or worse than Steve Wallace, but one thing he knew for sure was that Houston was no New York City. Schlegel tried to prove it on his next shot, when he struck again. Wallace stormed back with a crushing strike of his own.

Wallace gave Schlegel a chance to seize the lead when he left two pins standing on his next shot and converted the spare, but suddenly neither man could do enough to give the match away. Schlegel fumbled with a split on his next shot, then came so close to converting it that the crowd erupted with shrieks as he collapsed to his knees like a boy in the midst of desperate prayer. It was exactly the kind of misfortune that any budding champion stomped on, but instead Wallace left a split of his own. He cast an anxious glance at the scoreboard overhead to survey the damage done. He sighed, slumped his shoulders, and dropped his head.

"This is really the tell-tale shot, you might say, of this match," Welu explained as Schlegel rubbed his gloved right hand on his pants, stepped up to the approach, and inserted his fingers into his ball for the next shot. "Ernie Schlegel needs this strike to put the pressure on young Steve Wallace."

Wallace may have been young, but the kid had game. And Schlegel knew it.

It was shots like these that Schlegel had thrown so many times before, dancing on the razor's edge of a match with nearly enough money on the line to support a family for a year. But that was back in the poorly lit and seedy bowling alleys of New York City. Here in Buffalo under the TV lights, he would have to learn to close the deal under the glare of millions of viewers.

Schlegel stood and stared down his target with those narrowing eyes and began his shot, falling to one knee at the foul line as soon as he let the ball off his hand. He looked like a kid who was about to spring a diamond ring on the woman he meant to marry. He threw the ball harder than any shot he had made. It was the shot of a man who was not just looking to win; he was looking to kill. The ball blew through the pins, and then Schlegel got his first taste of the sting he would have to learn to savor if he was ever going to make it on tour. A single pin withstood the pounding.

This is a photo from the 1963 American Bowling Congress National Tournament, now known as the United States Bowling Congress Open Championships. Back in the day, this was *the* tournament at which to prove yourself. This photo features a young Kenny Barber standing by the ball return on lane 13, about to set up for his next shot. If you glance up at the score-board, you can see that Barber has four strikes in a row. Only one other player has strung together that many strikes. *Photo courtesy of Kenny Barber/the United States Bowling Congress.*

The Schlegels weeks after Ernie won the 1996 Masters.
Photo courtesy of Cathy Schlegel.

Schlegel with Toru Nagai, the Japanese restauranteur who drove Schlegel throughout New York City and beyond in his black Cadillac, looking for fish wherever they could be found. *Photo courtesy of Cathy Schlegel.*

The apartment building on Sickles Street in Inwood where Schlegel grew up. Schlegel's father, William, the superintendent of the building, would make him sweep those stairs clean every evening before he was allowed to eat dinner. *Photo courtesy of Gianmarc Manzione.*

Schlegel's parents, William and Irma.
Photo courtesy of Cathy Schlegel.

Schlegel making his debut on national TV as the Bicentennial Kid (ABC network) at Fair Lanes in Towson, Maryland. *Photo courtesy of Cathy Schlegel/Professional Bowlers Association.*

On the left, a late-career Schlegel bowling on ESPN in the 1990s, striking one of his inimitable poses at the foul line. *Photo courtesy of the United States Bowling Congress, provided by Cathy Schlegel.* On the right, Schlegel snarling en route to victory over Pete Weber at the 1985 Lite Beer Open. *Photo courtesy of the Professional Bowlers Association, provided by Cathy Schlegel.*

Schlegel celebrated his 70th birthday by—what else?—winning a poker tournament for $300. This is a shot of him at the poker table after the win. Bertha Krieg and Nat Rook are seated with Ernie at the Phoenix Casino in the Last Frontier Poker Room. *Photo courtesy of Cathy Schlegel and Ben Tracy.*

This photo captures the euphoric moment when Schlegel finally put 12 years of hard luck and hope behind him by winning his first Professional Bowlers Association title in 1980 at the King Louie Open against the great Bo Burton Jr., himself a legendary action bowler. Seconds after this photo was shot, Schlegel's wife threw him a stuffed monkey. He kissed it and threw it back. They enjoyed that monkey-off-his-back imagery. *Photo courtesy of Cathy Schlegel/Professional Bowlers Association.*

Schlegel bowling another telecast on ABC in 1983 at Garden City Bowl in Long Island. This shot captures Schlegel's unique intensity. *Photo courtesy of Cathy Schlegel/Professional Bowlers Association.*

The late, great Kenny Barber. Barber was one of the greatest bowlers—and greatest performers—in the history of action bowling. *Photo courtesy of Kenny Barber.*

This photo features Larry Lichstein, who was one of a very few people to clean out Kenny Barber in an action match at Central Lanes in Yonkers to the tune of $6,000 one night back in the mid-1960s. Larry says he knew from that night forward that he had found the thing he would do for the rest of his life. He even went on to become Rookie of the Year on the PBA Tour in 1969. *Photo courtesy of Luby Publishing.*

Side of the building that once housed Manhattan Lanes, Schlegel's home as a kid. This is the sidewalk where the bloody brawl between Schlegel and Ginsberg ensued in 1962. *Photo courtesy of Gianmarc Manzione.*

The Schlegels renewing their wedding vows on their 10th anniversary in 1985.
Photo courtesy of Cathy Schlegel.

One of the most devastating action bowlers—and an insatiable gambler—Richie Hornreich (left) accepting the first-place prize for winning the 12th Annual Vargo Classic in 1968. On rainy days, Hornreich would take bets on which raindrop would slide down the windows the fastest at Bay Ridge Lanes in Brooklyn. Standing next to Hornreich, on the right, is John Vargo, the tournament's namesake and the man who ensured his pins would be harder to knock over by filling them with lead. *Photo courtesy of United States Bowling Congress.*

Schlegel liked to wear vibrant colors on television. He called it "color therapy." The more aggressive the colors in his clothes were, the more aggressively he believed he would bowl. Whatever works, right? This particular photo was taken at the 1983 American Bowling Congress Masters, now a "major" on the PBA Tour. Ernie won the Masters in 1996 at age 53. To this day, he remains the oldest player ever to win a major on the PBA Tour. *Photo courtesy of Luby Publishing.*

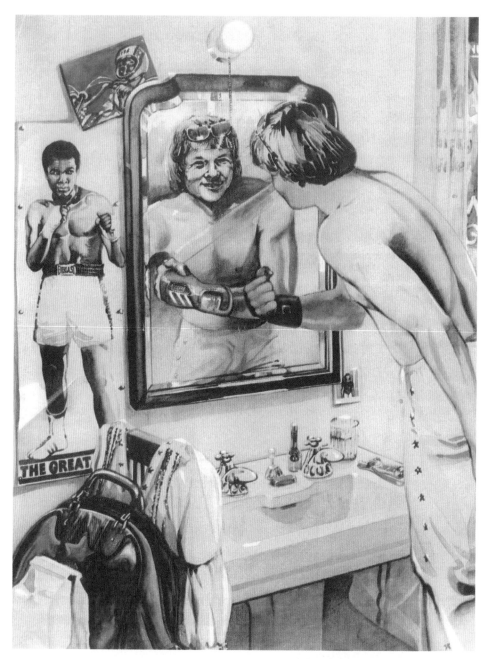

Illustration from the June 1979 issue of *Oui* magazine. Some items of note: The Muhammad Ali poster left of the mirror is an allusion to Schlegel's admiration for Ali, his idol. You see a small photo of Cathy, Schlegel's wife, to the lower-right of the mirror. You also see Schlegel's Bicentennial Kid costume slung over the back of a chair, and Schlegel's colorful bowling bag, designed by his wife. You also see Schlegel wearing his then-trademark white pants dotted with silver stars from hip to ankle, and his patented aviator shades. Additionally, you see a portrait of Evel Knievel in the upper-left. That's the person who inspired Schlegel's Bicentennial Kid gimmick. *Illustration courtesy of Frans Evenhuis.*

This photo captures Steve Harris meeting up with Schlegel at a pro bowling event nearly half-a-century removed from their days as two of New York City's preeminent bowling hustlers. They both have done quite well for themselves since their days on the streets. *Photo courtesy of Steve Harris.*

The chicken shack that currently occupies the site of Steve Harris's old pro shop at 4840 Broadway on the corner of Broadway and Academy in upper Manhattan. *Photo courtesy of Gianmarc Manzione.*

In 2014, Ernie Schlegel joined the 40-year participation club at the prestigious United States Bowling Congress Open Championships, a tournament that has been running for more than 100 years. *Photo courtesy of the United States Bowling Congress.*

"Well, it looked good!" Jackson said, baffled.

"Yes it did, Keith," Welu says. "The only thing is he might have had a little too much roll."

A little too much roll. Five years of waiting aimlessly on the streets of Inwood and soaping down AC units in Hackensack to enter the most revered arena the sport had to offer—the nationally televised finals of a PBA tournament—and all it took was "a little too much roll" to nudge him back onto the sidelines of his dreams. Now he was merely a hopeful onlooker again, merely another dreamer.

Wallace went on to clobber the next two bowlers, including Billy Hardwick, who was then in the midst of one of the most sensational winning streaks the PBA had ever seen, winning a total of seven titles in 1969 alone. His record would stand for the next decade.

Wallace then lost to Dick Ritger in the title match. He would have nothing to be ashamed of, as Ritger would go on to become a Hall of Famer and one of the game's greatest teachers. For a nineteen-year-old kid who dropped out of college in his sophomore year to see if he could hack it against the big guns on the lanes, Wallace's performance in Buffalo was one of the gutsiest efforts that fans of pro bowling had ever witnessed.

But there is no such thing as a consolation prize in professional sports. You either win or you lose. There is no gray area between greatness and mediocrity. If greatness is measured by the number of times a man weathers heartbreak to come back and try again, Schlegel soon would prove himself to be the most determined man in PBA history.

5

THE BICENTENNIAL KID

Nothing cures a sore hamstring like a well-rolled fatty and a dream. Back in a motel room in Buffalo after another lousy round of competition on the 1975 PBA Tour, six years after his debut in Buffalo, Schlegel stuffed and rolled another joint as he lamented a hamstring that felt like a stab wound and a career that seemed more like a curse. The man who never doubted that bowling would be his ride to freedom and recognition began to suspect, for the first and perhaps the only time in his life, that he might be the victim of a tragic overestimation of his own abilities.

Many thoughts crowded Schlegel's mind every time he stepped up to the approach to make another shot. He thought about that sore hammy and how close it might be to snapping and ending his career for good. He thought about the cruel deck of cards his body was dealing him at precisely the moment when everything felt like a new start—the divorce he had just finalized, the debts he had paid off, the second shot at life he thought he was about to seize. He thought about those dead-end jobs he took after an unexceptional debut on tour in 1968 sent him back to the streets of New York City penniless and looking for a way to support his young wife and baby daughter. How dreadful it was to consider that he may have to subject himself once again to those long nights behind the wheel of a cab, or those muggy summers unloading trucks for Coca-Cola, or those air-conditioning units he soaped down out in Hacken-sack. Jobs that made him feel only half alive. Now, years from all that and still looking for his first PBA title, he faced one of life's fundamental cruelties: The dreams you chase easily can turn to nightmares should you dare to pursue them.

In fact, 1975 turned out to be Schlegel's worst year on tour. Something had to give; he needed a perk.

Even Schlegel could not have known how appropriate it was that he found that perk by looking himself in the mirror. In just a few years' time, he no longer would recognize the man he saw there. With the smoke of his joint spiraling into the stale air, Schlegel stood and turned to the mirror. He did not know that what he would see there would change his life forever, but this was the moment he would refer to as the "vision" that reignited his career.

What he saw in that mirror brought him back to the ravaged apartment on Sickles Street where he lived as a bachelor. He heard the blasting Isley Brothers tune that rattled the walls after a concerned friend, Pete Mylenki, showed up to offer him that job out in Hackensack. He saw Evel Knievel jumping Snake River Canyon in his star-spangled costume and cape. He saw the Four Tops taking the stage in sequined suits and sparking smiles as Levi Stubbs swiveled toward the microphone for another booming take on "I Can't Help Myself," the euphoric crowd throbbing to the beat.

By the time he stood and stared into the mirror in that motel room, he knew exactly how he would let people know he was around. In the flash of that moment he met the legend he would become. He knew every seam and hem in the costumes he would wear. He knew the sequins that would adorn them, the aviator shades he would sport. He knew it all.

The man who stood before a motel room mirror that day was the first-generation son of a superintendent who discovered in the 200th anniversary of his country's birth an opportunity to become the legend he always felt he would be, a real-life comic book hero vanquishing enemies from coast to coast in his star-spangled get-up. If winning titles the way legendary peers such as Earl Anthony or Dick Weber did would not be his path to celebrity, then maybe this other way would work—this other self he saw in the mirror, this American hero.

To Schlegel, bowling was a boxing match, a spectacle viewers expect to entertain them. So many players on the PBA Tour in 1975 bowled the show in drab slacks and wooden hair with the expressionless countenance of the dead. That was about to change. The vision weed afforded him in that Buffalo motel room included more than shades and sequins and the passions they might provoke. It also included a redheaded woman. He had no idea who it was, or what she was doing there.

In September, 1975, at a PBA Tour stop in Detroit's Hartfield Lanes, twenty-four-year-old Catherine DePace scoured the bleachers behind the lanes for a seat where she could get a good view of the action. What she found instead was a seat next to the man she would marry weeks later. Then engaged in a souring relationship with another tour player named Mark Roth, DePace knew enough about the PBA to recognize Schlegel in those bleachers. She also recognized the empty seat next to him.

"Is that seat open, Ernie?" she asked.

Schlegel eyed the trim, stunning redhead who asked the question and gleefully answered in the affirmative. He soon discovered more to be happy about than DePace's looks. He discovered she, too, was a New York City kid. That she was an artist with a taste for fashion and design. The product of a family full of architects, DePace was a painter and a photographer then seeking to start her own graphics company and get her foot in the door with *House and Garden Magazine*. Within minutes, she knew the details of Schlegel's "vision" so comprehensively it was as if she had been renting space somewhere inside of it long before she met him. What she did not yet realize was that she indeed had spent time inside of it. That of all the bizarre props in the fantasy Schlegel indulged back in Buffalo that day, it was the mysterious redhead he remembered most vividly. And now the mystery was in the seat beside him. This was no fantasy now; this was his life. They left the bleachers for the lounge and kept talking.

The sequined suits, the aviator shades, the moniker to match the occasion of the nation's bicentennial, the rich man Schlegel planned to be when it was over and the many heads he planned to turn in the meantime—DePace listened to it all in a smoky lounge at the bowling center amid the din of crashing pins that would become the backdrop of their lives. She listened with the ear of an artist, but she also listened with the ear of a hardnosed kid from the same tough streets where Schlegel watched heroin strike down his friends with the efficiency of a wartime draft. In DePace, Schlegel found someone who learned as early as he did that the only way a kid gets by in a town like that is on guts and grit alone. The pills and weed so prevalent that those who did not partake were outcasts, the street gangs loitering around their local candy stores, the fine line between a life doomed by drugs and a life worth living—none of that was new to Cathy. At age seventeen, DePace phoned her father one day to inform him she would not be coming back home. She got by hauling paint brushes and buckets from apartment to apartment by subway, and painting living room walls for fifty bucks a pop, the kind of work DePace expected to come of the day she shared as many ideas as cigarettes with the dreamer she met in Detroit—another way to make a living. She would paint a few bowling bags. She would sew some sequins onto a shirt. Maybe when it was done she would have a few extra bucks to spare after paying the rent. It was her against the city streets. She'd follow a dollar wherever it may lead. It had led Cathy to the living rooms of locals whose walls needed painting, to the offices at Madison Square Garden where she put in her best effort as another nine-to-fiver in the accounting department, to this lounge chair at a bowling alley bar in Detroit.

She told Schlegel about the graphics company she had started with her brother, Joe. She handed him her business card and told him to get in touch when he was back in town. Cathy thought she merely had made another business deal that day. Three days later he showed up at her place with a toothbrush and a pair of socks in an overnight bag and absolutely no intention of leaving. They would be engaged that night. Money was going to be tight in a union between a starving artist and a struggling bowler, but that didn't matter to Cathy.

"People say that when you fall in love, that kind of stuff doesn't matter," Cathy recalled of the money she didn't have back then. "I could have lived with Schlegel in a dumpster."

They did have enough money to get hitched that December at the courthouse in time to make it out to the next PBA Tour stop together. All Schlegel had for a wedding ring was the one his sister gave him to put on Cathy's finger. The ring formerly belonged to his mother. The wedding rings and the money they didn't have to buy one were minor details to a couple of dreamy kids at the dawn of their life together. All that mattered now was that Schlegel had an appointment with destiny, the perfect woman at his side to help him get there, and an utter lack of fear before the immensity of his ambition. Schlegel and Cathy were done talking about the future. Now, it was time to make it happen.

Two months later, at the 1976 Fair Lanes Open in a Baltimore suburb called Towson, they made it happen. Schlegel bowled well enough to qualify for the championship round on ABC. It would be his first appearance on national TV as the newly minted the Bicentennial Kid. He and Cathy squeezed into the bowling alley locker room, and with ten minutes to go before airtime, they assembled the superhero Schlegel saw in the mirror back in Buffalo.

Schlegel put on his aviator shades. He stepped into his snow-white pair of pants dotted with a stripe of silver studs strung down the side of each leg from waist to ankle. He pushed his arms into the ruffled sleeves of a V-neck top glittering with white and blue sequins. His collar sparkled with silver stars that converged in the center of his chest, exposing a vague patch of chest hair and a gold necklace as thin as lace. He finished off the costume with a pair of red, white, and blue bowling shoes.

The Bicentennial Kid was born.

"He must have known he was going to make the show, because he was all prepared," ABC commentator Bo Burton said of Schlegel and his costume on the show that afternoon.

Schlegel did indeed know he would make the show. Now that he had his costume, in fact, he was so certain he would make the show that Cathy hurriedly put the finishing touches on his outfit during the drive to the tournament. Schlegel still had more than forty grueling games of competition ahead of him at that point with no guarantee of even making any money, no less of making the show. But in his mind, before he threw his first shot that week, he had already vanquished the field. This was a confidence Schlegel never before enjoyed.

Nothing provided Schlegel with a more powerful incentive to succeed than his costume. Not the paychecks he hoped to sign his name to by the end of the week. Not the trophy he hoped to hoist above his head as he smiled for reporters' cameras. Nothing. It was the clothes he bowled for now, the adrenaline of that moment when he burst on the set with his red and blue sequins sparkling under the lights to the crowd's ovation. No one in the history of the PBA—then nearly twenty years old—had seen anything like this before. If ratings were what ABC wanted for its weekly bowling show, ratings were exactly what Schlegel would deliver. As it was, pro bowling's ratings already provided Schlegel with a platform that reached 20 million viewers. In the mid 1970s, PBA's broadcasts out-rated Major League Baseball, professional basketball, and pro golf's Masters. They also rivaled college basketball's NCAA tournament. This was the opportunity Schlegel had envisioned in that motel room mirror as he dreamed his way out of despair, the moment he knew he would share with Cathy before he had even seen her face.

But Schlegel was the fourth seed on the show. If this moment was going to last much longer, he first would have to beat one of the greatest bowlers who ever lived. His opponent in the opening match was fifth seed Billy Hardwick.

Hardwick was a blond-haired California kid who stunned the bowling world in 1969 when he set the record for most titles in a single season—seven. Hardwick had it all by then—starring in television commercials for Miller High Life, thrashing all comers from the United States to Japan and back, and landing enough endorsements to rival the earnings of other stars of the day such as Mickey Mantle.

All the fame and glory that came his way by 1969 turned out to be the dream before the nightmare of his life. Within three years, Hardwick would lose two infant sons—one to Sudden Infant Death Syndrome (SIDS) and the other to a complicated pregnancy that culminated in a premature birth from which the baby died. He went the next seven years without a single title, and his life would never be the same. But in 1976, Hardwick was in the midst of a career resurgence that saw him qualify for the televised finals several times that season and come within a single game of winning the coveted Firestone Tournament of Champions title.

When he faced Schlegel from across a ball return to shake his hand before the opening match of the 1976 Fair Lanes Open, no one in Billy Hardwick's life, least of all Hardwick himself, was smiling. His mother-in-law had just recently been laid to rest, and his wife back home felt scorned by a distant Hardwick's return to the road as she grieved. By then, Hardwick was a man who knew that any loss he may face on the lanes would be no match for the losses he had endured away from them. He had faced the deaths of his sons and the pieces of himself that died along with them, the death of his once-soaring career, and now the death of his mother-in-law and the fear that his second marriage could be next.

DePace, now Cathy Schlegel, and her costumed husband opened the locker room door to walk the narrow pathway between towering bleachers on their way to the set.

"Are you ready, honey?" Schlegel asked.

They had a lot to be ready for by then: their new life together, the thrills and heartbreaks the PBA Tour life would impart, the unending struggle to make enough money on tour to keep bowling for a living, this show where Schlegel's costume would make him the hero or the fool. Imagine showing up dressed as bowling's own Evel Knievel and proceeding to embarrass yourself by bowling a lousy game before a national audience of millions?

Schlegel ran down the aisle with raised fists. He needed the crowd on his side after Hardwick made his entrance onto the set to be introduced as the fifth seed. They knew Hardwick had made a furious charge to make the show. The man had just roared back from a deficit seemingly too significant to overcome in order to qualify for the championship round. And some knew about the horrors Hardwick had bowled through all these years since that dream season back in '69. The crowd greeted Hardwick with an ovation. For a moment, at least, Hardwick was the fan favorite.

Only those in attendance saw the boisterous entrances that occurred moments before the show went to air. Those who tuned in later saw an enraptured crowd applauding noisily as play-by-play announcer Bud Palmer struggled against the din to conduct his opening segment. The crowd wasn't screaming for Earl or Weber or Hardwick. They screamed for Schlegel.

The crowd was speckled with women in beehive hairdos and men in checkered pants and bushy sideburns that placed them unmistakably in the time capsule that was the 1970s. And all of them, hipsters and squares alike, were rapt in the thrill of what they just saw. Clearly, something happened before Palmer took his place in front of the camera. This was something bigger than a bowling tournament, something the writhing crowd in the stands behind Palmer's head would not soon forget.

Palmer introduced his broadcast partner and PBA champion Nelson "Bo" Burton Jr., who stepped into the camera's view giggling as if someone told him a bawdy joke on his way over. They were dressed in wool blazers the color of the sun and just as blinding to look at, with wide lapels and ABC's lower-case insignia emblazoned on the right breast pocket in black lettering. With their sport coats and made-for-TV tans, they looked like a couple of lemon popsicles melting under the TV lights. Burton's sideburns reached halfway down his face and the jet-black pile of hair on his head almost resembled the shape of a wasp's nest. He wore a powder-blue shirt with an auburn tie that had a floral print. His brawny arms highlighted the chiseled figure he cut as a power-lifting gym rat.

Palmer and Burton were in for a show that day. That much, clearly, was certain.

Hardwick showed up in a pair of aqua-blue polyester pants printed with white patchwork squares and an ivory-white vinyl belt around his waist. It was the era of the leisure suit and bushy hair. Hardwick, formerly known at the pinnacle of his glory as "the blond bomber," sported thick locks of straight, strawberry-blond hair that gushed down the sides of his head. He wore a cerulean polo shirt with a chalk-white collar, a black leather glove with cut-off fingers on his bowling hand, and a glittering Rolex around his left wrist. Plum-dark marks cradled his eyes like a couple of fading half-moons. They sank into his doughy face as he leered threateningly at the pins for his first shot, and held his amber bowling ball chin-high before making his first step toward the foul line. Hardwick may have had a lot to bowl for, but nonetheless he stumbled out of the gate with an eight-count and a spare to open the match.

That was when the show within the show began. Schlegel stepped up for his first shot on national television as the Bicentennial Kid. It was his first shot of the match, but it was also his first shot at the stardom he intended to seize, the first of many appearances he would make on ABC in 1976. More than anything, this was the first shot of the rest of his career. His red and blue sequins sparkled under the lights of the set; they ran straight up the front of his white top in double lines that enclosed a single row of silver stars, then over his shoulders and down his back like a pair of suspenders. His sleeves were ruffled from elbow to hand and ringed at the wrist with sequins, and the bush of blond hair on his head was so thick it looked like a shrub that had not been sheared in months. The lights of TV cameras cast a glare on his amber shades as he looked up at the pins and took a deep breath with a poker player's deadpan demeanor.

"And look at this outfit now as we go to Ernie Schlegel," Palmer noted as Schlegel stood on the approach and inserted his fingers into a jet-black bowling ball with three white dots printed across the finger holes like a string of pearls. "That's why he calls himself the Bicentennial Kid. It's a little bit like maybe something Evel Knievel might wear."

"That's Evel Ernie, Bud," Bo Burton said with a chuckle. "Ernie Schlegel."

"He says he doesn't come from any town, just the good ol' U.S.A.," Palmer noted.

Palmer and Burton's bemusement traced a fine line between disbelief and derision, precisely the line Cathy in particular hoped to avoid as she helped Schlegel into his costume in the locker room. She didn't want him to bowl a bad game. She was scared. She knew he could make or break their future in one game.

The only thing Schlegel broke when he threw his first shot was the rack of pins he stared down as Palmer and Burton exchanged quips about his raiment. Schlegel threw a perfect shot to blow all ten pins off the deck as if they were made of smoke. The crowd Schlegel owned the second he stepped onto the set went berserk. Then he stepped up and did it again. His second shot buried the pocket with such force that one pin tomahawked another in the opposite corner and sent it flying.

Hardwick may have called California home as a kid, but in 1976 he hailed from Louisville, Kentucky, a residence that inspired its host of monikers just as California did back when he was known as "the boy with the golden claw." Now he was known as "Bluegrass Billy."

His blond hair fluttered over the gush of air blowing out of the ball return while Burton described him for the TV audience as "quite a performer."

A performer Hardwick may have been, but after two more bumbling shots that prompted commentary from Burton on how low the scores had been all week, it appeared as if he may have forgotten his script back in his hotel room.

Then the show within the show resumed. Schlegel returned to the approach for his third shot.

"We've got a real hot pistol here in the Bicentennial Kid. I just love that outfit! You have to be some kind of an extrovert to wear that!" Palmer said as Burton burst into laughter. "I'd like to buy one for you if you would wear it."

"Well, I wish I could get on the show to wear it, Bud!" responded Burton, a legendary bowler himself.

The top Cathy had tried to lengthen with sequins now exposed Schlegel's lower back as he bent at the foul line to deliver his third shot of the match. Right off his hand the ball appeared to be left of his target, meandering over to the wrong side of the headpin. For a second it seemed Schlegel had thrown an errant shot to give Hardwick a breather, and that was when he dazzled the crowd with an improbable strike. The ball crossed over to the left pocket and wiped all ten pins off the deck for a lucky break. It was his third consecutive strike to open the match. The crowd unleashed a deafening roar. He then stepped up and devastated the pocket in the third and fourth frames. Four shots, four strikes. He did it again in the sixth frame and found himself halfway home to a rare, televised perfect game, swinging his fist so hard as he returned to his seat that his mop of blond hair quaked over his forehead. He grabbed his ball rag off the ball return and took his seat as Hardwick rose for his next shot. The camera panned the crowd and spotted Cathy. She applauded and laughed, nodding her head as if she simply could not believe what she was witnessing. A subtle shade of rouge reddened her ivory cheeks to match her wine-red hair. She sported a patterned, sepia shirt with the top button undone to expose a necklace of brown and beige beads clinging to her neck. It was an elegance one would expect more of an artist on her way to a Soho fashion show in New York City than someone in attendance at a bowling tournament. But this was the 1970s, when people dressed as well to board a plane as they did to attend a friend's wedding, and even the men who showed up in suits and ties for a seat behind the lanes were not out of place. A dear friend of the Schlegels, U.S. Air Force Officer, Larry Plecha, sat beside her in the stands. His presence there was the only thing in the house that could calm her racing pulse.

Schlegel proceeded to demolish Billy Hardwick, winning the match with a final score of 256. A single pin withstood another pocket shot in the seventh frame to blow his chances for a perfect game, but nothing could withstand the onslaught Schlegel delivered throughout the match. Not even that thoroughbred, Billy Hardwick. Hardwick gathered his ball and shoes and headed for the door, quipping along the way that the red-hot Schlegel needed "a saliva test."

Then a doomed former prodigy in the midst of a comeback stepped up to challenge Schlegel in the next match: Bobby Jacks, the third seed, and the pro tour's ultimate lost soul.

The first time anyone outside his native New Orleans heard of Bobby Jacks, he was lighting himself a cigarette somewhere in the pages of a mid-'60s issue of *Bowlers Journal*, on his way into a Bourbon Street Jazz club. A headline under the photo read "A Star in the Making," and with his pompadour hairdo and slick black tie, who could argue otherwise?

A gifted, left-handed action bowler who turned to gambling when his parents abandoned him at the age of eleven after they divorced, Jacks became known for walking with a cane and sporting pinkie rings and diamond cufflinks by age nineteen. By then, he had accomplished the near-impossible feat of winning three titles in a single PBA season. Some say the money came to Jacks too soon, but for Jacks it could not come soon enough. He was known as much for his brilliance on the lanes as for his lengthening rap sheet, doing stints in jail for writing bad checks.

The Bobby Jacks who stared across a ball return in Baltimore to shake hands with Schlegel for game two had traded his pompadour hairdo for a bushy perm long ago. A thick, black mustache obscured his upper lip, and the ravages of a hard-luck life left him with the leathered face of a man well beyond his twenty-nine years. A blood-red polo shirt and checkered pants replaced the suit and tie he sported on the streets of New Orleans back when he was the star and the world was his jazz joint. But here in Baltimore he was just the guy who had not won a title in ten years. It was Schlegel's world he inhabited now.

Schlegel stepped up and leered at the pins through his aviator shades for the first shot of the match. With his ruffled sleeves and sequined suit, Schlegel looked like someone who guided tigers through flaming hoops on the evening shift at Circus Circus. Some called him a clown; others called him crazy. But those who knew Schlegel best saw that he walked a fine line between lunacy and genius, a line he hoped to walk straight to the bank.

"When a player gets into what we call a 'dead stroke' on tour he can do almost anything," Burton said "But Schlegel's got a tough tiger on his hands with Bobby Jacks."

Tough as that tiger may have been, this was only his second time bowling a PBA telecast in the last ten years. It was a decade in which Jacks had lived many lives: The star in the making, the scared kid on the lam after going AWOL from the army, the fraudster in the pen after writing one too many bad checks. What memory he may have had of how to win was obscured by the haze of so much circumstance. And as he fell off balance and left two pins standing on his first shot, it seemed for a second that Jacks had no memory at all of the cocky kid with the pinkie rings and greased pompadour.

But a single frame does not a whole game make. Jacks collected himself for the second frame and splintered the rack for a strike. When he did it again in the fourth frame, taking the lead over Schlegel with his most devastating strike yet, Jacks seemed well on his way to leaving the past behind him.

Schlegel responded with three strikes in a row and Bo once again expressed his amazement at the Bicentennial Kid.

"Schlegel is bowling beautifully out there, Bud," Burton said. "Nobody has maintained a stroke like this all week. This is the way all the matches have gone most of the week, seesawing back and forth, very competitive."

Jacks never was much interested in seesaws. You don't get a lot of time in at the playground when you're thrown to the streets of New Orleans at age eleven, but you do learn what it takes to survive. That is precisely the statement Jacks made with his next shot, yet another thunderous strike that blew the pins into the pit so violently they seemed to dissolve before the viewer's eyes. Jacks was feeling it, the adrenaline that pushed him through three titles in a single summer back in '66, the memory of what it took to make more money in that handful of weeks than he had ever seen in his life. He would need the full measure of that moxie now, leading the match by three pins in the tenth frame and three strikes away from locking Schlegel out altogether.

With potentially $8,000 riding on the next shot—the prize he would bank if he won the title—Jacks decided to try his luck with some psychological gymnastics. He complained to PBA Tournament Director Harry Golden that the pins were not aligned properly and requested a re-rack. In pro bowling, a re-rack request is equivalent to calling a timeout as the field goal kicker's foot is a about to strike the football in the final few moments of a tied-up NFL game. Jacks may have seen a problem with the pins or he may have been full of it, but either way Schlegel had to sit through the delay and think a little longer about the high-pressure shot he had to make. What Jacks may not have understood, however, is that they may play those games down in New Orleans, but they invented those games up in New York City.

As tutored in the art of psychological warfare as any seasoned PBA player, Burton could not help but chuckle at the spectacle.

"The pins are probably in the same spot now as they were before the re-rack," he joked as the match resumed, "but in his mind they're different, and that's all that counts right now."

Maybe so. Or maybe the disastrous six-count Jacks got on his next shot revealed that the only guy he psyched out was himself. Despite Jacks's whiff in the tenth, Schlegel would still be loading up his car after this game if he failed to strike on his next shot. His last few shots on the lane where he must perform or go home had been poor—an open frame earlier in the game followed by a few spares.

"He can bowl for the next five weeks with the money he could make on this one shot," Burton said.

Money is nice, but respect is priceless. Winning is the only avenue to respect on the PBA Tour, and that is something no amount of money will buy. Schlegel gathered his ball and stepped up to the approach. He let out a huge sigh as he prepared to throw one do-or-die shot. A strike and the match was all but his. Anything less and the Bicentennial Kid would clear the stage for the Comeback Kid.

Finally, Schlegel took the first step of his shot after a long, focused pause. Someone in the crowd slammed a door; a loud squeak and slam pierced the crowd's hushed silence. Schlegel let the ball go nonetheless. It was a solid shot. Unlike the previous few he threw on this lane, this one seemed to have a chance when it cleared the arrows. Down went nine pins, while the ten pin in the corner only tilted slightly to the left. Then, as if blown over by a sudden breeze, it fell. Strike.

Schlegel scowled and swung his arm through the air in celebration as the crowd roared. But the first thing on his mind when he turned around to settle down for his next shot was that clueless bastard who slammed a damned door midway through the most important shot of his career. Schlegel squinted into the distance to spot the trouble, clearly consumed now by a baffling combination of rapture over the strike and utter rage at the perpetrator of the noise that almost snatched it from him.

With a nine-count and a spare, Schlegel would edge out Jacks's 214 game with a score of 215 and move on. But Schlegel stepped up and did one better—yet another strike for a 225 to vanquish Jacks and welcome PBA journeyman Curt Schmidt into the lion's cage Schlegel had paced in for two games now.

Jacks packed up and vanished into another decade of obscurity. He would resurface one last time in the TV finals of the 1986 Miller High Life Challenge, then disappear for good.

Schmidt and Schlegel belonged together about as much as a monk belongs in a brothel. The son of a Lutheran Minister, Schmidt was born in a town called Pekin, an obscure hamlet in upstate New York where the road signs outnumber the people; Schlegel was born in the biggest city in the world. Schmidt grew up bowling in an eight-lane center in Woodlawn, Indiana, where his family moved when he was twelve; Schlegel grew up bowling in every alley in New York City. Schmidt pitched horse shoes when he was not bowling; Schlegel's only experience with horses was throwing down a wad of cash on the trifecta at the racetrack. Schmidt spoke in a subdued Midwestern drawl that sounded as though he were falling asleep as he talked; Schlegel spoke in a tough Manhattan accent that sounded as though he were spitting nails. Schmidt loved to croon the Jim Nabors hit "Back Home in Indiana" at karaoke joints on the road; Schlegel grew up blasting Isley Brothers tunes at pot parties on the bad side of Broadway.

Yet it was the minister's son from Indiana, and not the hardnosed kid from tough streets, who already owned two PBA titles. Schlegel was just another winless dreamer and Schmidt was the battle-tested pro. With his receding hairline, obtrusive forehead and angular face, the five-foot-six Schmidt so closely resembled Ray Walston of *My Favorite Martian* fame that everyone on tour knew him only as "The Martian." But when he stepped onto the set in a pair of tan slacks and a lime polo shirt, buttoned to the chin, to shake hands with the foe in the sequined suit, the gaunt and graying forty-three-year-old looked more like the bewildered grandfather of a boy who had become the family outcast.

Schmidt's bewilderment turned to sheer incredulity when his first shot blew out the pocket, only to somehow leave a stunned corner pin standing. When it happened again and then yet again in the third and fourth frames, he slumped his head and sighed like a man who just got sacked from his job. This was neither bewilderment nor disbelief now. This was utter resignation.

Schlegel knew he had a match on his hands, maybe the toughest of the afternoon. He left splits in consecutive frames after a sloppy strike to open the game. The 256 he shot against Hardwick in game one felt like it had happened a year ago. He leaned off to the side with his legs crossed and one arm draped over the seat beside him, a casual manner that obscured the disgust contorting his mouth—the only outward expression of adversity he allowed. He cloaked any other evidence of emotion behind his aviator shades and that mop of strawberry-blond hair crouching around his head. It was the countenance of a poker player so skilled in masking the slightest uncertainty that he might as well be a pillar of stone.

If he betrayed no fear as he sat and waited for Schmidt to finish his shots, he damned sure would not let Schmidt see any sign of it as he bowled. Schlegel set up for his next shot, stared down the pins and promptly threw his finest shot of the game—"no doubt about that one!" Bud Palmer said—then strolled back to his seat as if he had merely dropped a letter in the mail.

An exasperated Schmidt, clearly still brooding over the brutal breaks of the past two frames, responded with two errant shots for spares. He turned, shaking his head, ripped his towel from the ball return, and seethed as he waited for his ball to come back between shots, his lead slipping away.

With a chance to take the lead with a strike, Schlegel nearly left another split and turned clutching his chest with a gasp as Burton and Palmer chuckled at his desperation. He picked up a rosin bag used to keep bowlers' hands dry during competition, and slammed it back down onto the ball return, gesticulating wildly in a fit of self-loathing. It was the body language of a man who knew that the longer you leave the door open for a pro the more likely he will be to walk right through it without so much as a "thank you." With a top prize of $8,000 on the line—a decent chunk of change in 1976—there was absolutely no room for error, no time for close calls and gasps.

Schmidt stepped up in the ninth frame with the game virtually tied. He threw a strike, twirled around and pumped his fist toward the ground on one knee like it was a bayonet he meant to jam through the gut of an enemy soldier. The streets may be meaner in New York City than they are in Indiana, but out on tour, every moment was a mean street where the money was scarce and the only way to get any was to fight for it. Every shot on tour was a cliff you dangled from. Everyone you faced was eager to push you over the edge.

If it was a boxing match Schlegel craved on the lanes, that was exactly what Curt Schmidt gave him now. Schlegel found himself playing Muhammad Ali to Schmidt's Joe Frazier, the flashy maverick tangling with the straitlaced grinder. As a huge fan of Ali, Schlegel knew there was a night when Frazier sent Ali home a loser, and the memory of that infamous fight came back to him now. Schlegel himself had lived through his own version of that night more times than he cared to remember— nights when he too went home the loser, when the one bad shot or tough break that did him in replayed itself in his mind like a bit of bad news he refused to believe. He did not want a night like that tonight.

It was too late for Schlegel to shut out Curt Schmidt now. The two splits he left early in the game made it mathematically impossible for him to lock Schmidt out completely, even if he threw nothing but strikes from now on. The game was Schmidt's to win or lose. But if Schlegel could find that same magic somewhere within himself that he found the night he threw the three best strikes Johnny Campbell ever saw, he would at least force Schmidt into needing a strike on his next shot to win. As Campbell learned that night, and as Bobby Jacks witnessed in Baltimore that afternoon, there was something about pressure that flipped a switch in Schlegel's mind, something about the adrenaline of the do-or-die shot that dissolved his fear. That was the Ernie Schlegel with whom Schmidt got acquainted now as he watched Schlegel throw his finest shot of the match on the first ball of the tenth frame. It was a flawless and explosive strike.

"Once again, Ernie Schlegel dynamic in the clutch," Burton says. "He has to have this next strike."

So here it was again. One more "has-to-have" moment behind him and another on the way. He wiped the lane oil off of his ball and breathed, his red and blue sequins sparkling under the TV lights.

Schlegel struck and twirled around with both arms flailing through the air. He collapsed onto one knee and swung his right hand across his body as if backhanding someone who had crossed him.

"Just a tremendous performance!" Bo Burton exclaimed as the crowd roared. "Schlegel has always been an aggressive player, and he's shown it right here. He has now forced Curt Schmidt to strike on his first ball of the tenth frame. He's thinking about eight thousand bucks right now. Ernie Schlegel—they're gonna call him 'Evel Schlegel' after today!"

All of those in attendance at Fair Lanes would remember the rebel in sequins and shades who threw strikes whenever circumstances required him to do so—and that, after all, was Schlegel's goal.

The applauding crowd whistled and shouted like front-row fans at an arena rock concert, begging the band for an encore. Whatever happened from this moment on, it was clear that something big had gone down at Fair Lanes—something the PBA never had seen before, something that promised to wrench professional bowling out of its world of pressed slacks and parted hair and into a future where attitude would become the new normal. If the future had a name, its name was Ernie Schlegel.

But no amount of guts or flash would shut the door Schlegel left open as he stumbled through the early frames of the match with two bad shots for splits. The crowd may have loved him, but crowds are fickle, and soon they could find themselves falling in love with the loser.

If it was possible for a country kid from Indiana to out-scrap a brawling gambler from mean streets, Curt Schmidt would have one shot to prove it now. And he would have to do it on the right-hand lane—the lane on which he had not yet thrown a strike.

The crowd continued to roar over Schlegel's clutch turkey. Burton strained to be heard over the din, explaining that "Curt Schmidt needs one strike to beat Ernie Schlegel."

Schmidt conferred with Harry Golden, demanding to have the pins re-racked just so he could buy himself some breathing time while the pins were being set. Schmidt wiped the sole of his left shoe—the sliding foot—with a lemon-colored towel, never once looking away from the pins he glared at as if they formed the face of an enemy. He shook a rosin bag in his bowling hand and waited. Maybe he even breathed once or twice as he stood and stared down the lane; maybe he hardly breathed at all.

Schlegel draped his arms across the chairs at each side of him, his legs crossed and his ruffled sleeves dangling from under his arms like flags sagging from a pole on a windless day. The stripe of silver stars strung up the legs of his snow-white pants sparkled under the lights. He adjusted the glove on his bowling hand as if to assure himself he would bowl one more game.

The crowd quieted to a hush as Schmidt gathered his ball and wiped it clean of lane oil with his yellow towel. He stepped up to the approach to throw his shot.

Schmidt threw his shot, pausing over the foul line with his bowling hand raised just over his eyes like a man trying to glimpse a far-off building through the fog. The ball cut sharply toward the pocket. Clearly this shot at least stood a chance of winning him the match as it sliced to the left. And then it happened. The ball blasted all ten pins into the pit, and the country kid from Indiana pulled the curtain on the show the Bicentennial Kid had put on for the past three games. Schmidt twirled around and collapsed to one knee as he pumped his fist and held it there.

"That is a winning shot, Bud!" Burton shouted over the crowd's ovation.

The camera panned quickly to Schlegel to find him picking up his bowling balls from the ball return and packing them away after having shaken Schmidt's hand in defeat. The PBA Tour's TV shows provide bowlers with little time to sulk on the set. Another match awaits; the show must go on. The vanquished must gather their things and go.

Even as Burton and Palmer knew Schmidt was the man who would move on from here, it was Schlegel's performance, and not Schmidt's gutsy strike, that they could not stop talking about. Palmer noted that Schmidt would face top seed Dave Davis in the final match almost as an afterthought, and then he offered a final and emphatic note of praise for Schlegel.

"Tremendous pressure bowling by Ernie Schlegel," he said as the show cut into a commercial break.

Anyone who had seen the show knew that this mop-headed hero would show his face on their TV screens again. More than knowing it, they would hope for it. Whether those who tuned into ABC that afternoon loved or hated what they saw, they wanted to see it again. That was a minor victory no one could take away from him.

6

THE GORILLAS OF VANCOUVER

Minor victories were fine in 1976. After all, Schlegel did make it onto more TV shows that year than at any time in his career, find the woman of his dreams, and prove to the world that he belonged on tour. But by 1979, he was three years deeper into his career and he still had not a single title to show for it. It was time for an actual victory, not the pyrrhic one he enjoyed that day back at the Fair Lanes Open in Baltimore. It was time to answer the gathering chorus of questions surrounding him.

"I really hope that Schlegel wins a pro title, and soon," Larry Lichstein, then working as the Director of Player Services for the PBA, wrote in *Bowlers Journal* at the end of the 1978 season. "Why? Because he's paid his dues. Schlegel's had his chance to win on several occasions, but something always managed to go wrong. However, the fact that he got into those title matches was no fluke. The man's a tremendous bowler."

That was the question: Why was this "tremendous bowler" not winning? Where was the scowling kid from Upper Manhattan who pounded his chest like a gorilla as he defied all comers one summer day at Central Lanes in Yonkers, a gush of Vaseline melting out of his hair in the heat? Where was the Ernie Schlegel who shoved his raw fingers into those blood-stained holes and threw the best three strikes Johnny Campbell ever saw? When would that Ernie Schlegel please stand up and take a bow? By 1979, people began to lose hope that that winner would ever show his face on tour.

"Some call him the greatest non-champion of them all," wrote bowling historian and co-founder of the PBA, Chuck Pezzano, that year. "Others are not so kind when the name Ernie Schlegel enters the conversation. The words apple, choke and flake are tossed around loosely."

The only conversation anyone was having on the PBA Tour at the time surrounded one name: Mark Roth. As Schlegel chased an elusive first title for more than a decade, he watched Roth pace him twenty-two times in a four-year stretch from '75-'79. A stocky, fearless kid from Brooklyn who had the stare of a killer and threw the ball like a cannon, Roth grew up storming some of the same smoky action bowling haunts as Schlegel, leaving stories in his wake that would be told for decades to come. There was the time he busted out of a bowling alley at twenty-two years old with $4,500 and showed up in a new Dodge the next day; the time he threw a bowling ball through the floor in fury; the time he got married in a New York Ranger's jersey; the night he converted the virtually impossible 7-10 split.

The pioneer of something known in bowling as a "power game," Roth's stomping steps resembled a stampede of startled buffalo as he charged toward the foul line. He kept his wrist cocked under the ball as it exploded out of his hand and whipped back toward the pocket to obliterate the pins. It was a ferocity never before seen in the sport, a physical dominance that had many opposing players beaten before they threw a ball, so intimidating was Roth's presence.

Roth's ability to transform bowling balls into bombs came at the expense of a thumb that rarely endured the stress without bleeding—a thumb that became as much of a myth as the man himself. Whenever Roth's thumb bled, it filled with pus, putting him out of commission until the swelling receded. Schlegel referred to himself as Roth's "doctor," and would "build" Roth a thumb from the gnarled mess it became, repairing it with a liquid bandage called Nu-Skin to the point where Roth still could bowl well enough to qualify for the televised finals. Many who watched Roth develop as one of Brooklyn's emerging players told him he would never make it throwing the ball that way. Within a few years, no one remembered the names of those doubters, but everyone knew the name of Mark Roth.

Ironically, Roth also happened to be Cathy Schlegel's last boyfriend. At that time, Catherine DePace had been twenty-four years old and ready for more, but the only marriage Mark Roth was interested in was the one between him and the lanes that would make him famous. Enter Ernie Schlegel and the tournament in Detroit where he turned to find Cathy sitting next to him. She was ready for a starring role and feared she would never find it with Roth. Schlegel was her answer, and soon he became her husband.

Now it was Roth, and not Schlegel, who was dominating the pro tour. As Cathy watched Roth break Billy Hardwick's record for most titles won in a single season—eight, which he won in 1978—she could not help but wonder why Roth was winning a title virtually every week, but Schlegel had not yet won at all. To anyone who had witnessed what Schlegel was capable of in the early days when he and Roth were a couple of

New York City kids, it didn't make sense. Schlegel was making money on tour; he just was not making good on his dream to become a PBA champion. What tour money he pocketed in the meantime was like sand passing through his fingers. It was barely enough to make rent and child support payments. By 1979, Schlegel needed more than just "a perk." He needed to become a bonafide champion.

By 1979, the Schlegels had moved to Vancouver, Washington, to live near the headquarters of the Contour Power Grips company. Schlegel had signed on to sell the company's "grips"—rubber inserts placed inside finger holes to give a bowler more lift on a shot and help generate more power and revolutions on the ball. Schlegel's quirky personality and fairly routine appearances on national television soon would prove to be a goldmine for the company. Every time he paused on the approach to set up for a shot on TV, he made sure to hold his bowling ball in such a position that the grips in his finger holes were in plain view of the camera. He went on to move millions of units for Contour, hawking bags full of grips from tour stop to tour stop, working the phones, and adding pro-shop proprietors from coast to coast to his burgeoning list of clients. His partnership with Contour would endure for nearly twenty years.

Before the 1979 season, he found something else in Vancouver: a man who made champions. Gery Gehrmann was a 6'2" ox of a human being with the build of a hunter who carries home the deer he shot on his back. A member of both the local and national amateur wrestling halls of fame who played tackle for Washington State in the early 1960s, Gehrmann had leathery hands the size of catcher's mitts. In addition to his duties as gym teacher at the local high school, Gehrmann also served as football coach. He imposed two easy rules on his students: no fighting, and no cursing. When one kid decided it would be a good idea to kick another square in the balls, Gehrmann pulled the kids apart.

"Get your hands off of me, or I'll sue you!" the kid told Gehrmann.

Gehrmann's eyes, two blue beads pinched into his gigantic bull's head, tightened.

"All right," he told the kid, "you get the first swing, and then I'll break your neck!"

"I won't do it again, sir!" the kid squeaked.

Any way you looked at it, Gehrmann was tough. He had recently undergone two angioplasties and was already running the seven-mile stretch between school and home again. After his incredible rebound from the heart attack—the first of four he would survive in his life—he carried himself with the confidence of a man who knew he had done something no one ever could take away from him. Schlegel himself thirsted for that kind of confidence, and put himself in Gehrmann's hands. The first thing Gehrmann did was to replace the four packs of cigarettes Schlegel smoked each day with a fitness regimen so grueling that the first day left him writhing in the street like a fresh scrap of road kill.

"What did he do to you! What did he do!" Cathy screamed the day she found Schlegel crawling home on all fours after a preliminary workout with Gehrmann. He had just completed his first seven-mile run up and down the hills of Vancouver.

"I don't know," Schlegel said, "but it hurts!"

It was the sort of pain generally reserved for two types of people: inmates of seventeenth century asylums in France or people who stand in front of speeding trains. Naturally, then, Schlegel showed up bright and early to endure the fullest extent of this agony day after day. In Gehrmann, Schlegel found a drill sergeant so schooled in the benefits of self-inflicted punishment that his high school gym students became known collectively as "Gehrmann's Gorillas." Gehrmann honored their tolerance for pain with a sign outside their workout area that read: "Gehrmann's Gorillas: Please Do Not Feed the Animals." Here was a zoo Schlegel eagerly wished to join at a time in his career when an unflattering designation as the PBA Tour's "greatest non-champion"—the bowler who had earned the most money in PBA Tour winnings without claiming a single title—plagued him. Schlegel was looking to win, and Gehrmann knew it.

"Greatest Non-Champion." Nothing softened the sting of that phrase. To be a "non-champion," great or not, was—in Schlegel's mind—to be a loser. And to be a loser was to commit to a failure for which he could never forgive himself, the failure to live up to an admonishment from his father that he never forgot all those years ago, when he stood before a judge with a gaggle of pocketbook-snatching kids from his block.

The word around tour may well have been that Schlegel choked in big matches. But the word inside Schlegel's head was that he was a winner—a Schlegel. That no one on the PBA Tour could out-bowl him one-on-one—including Roth—and that if he had to die trying to prove it, then Gehrmann and his Gorillas would be happy to help him do just that. If those roads found Schlegel crawling home after a seven-mile run, well, that was how it went when you knocked on the door of the Gorillas' training ground looking for a spot in their "zoo." You either did what it took to be great, or you did nothing at all. You may have come within an inch of your life a few days into the first week, but if you somehow lived to see those hard days through, you were already well on your way to overcoming yourself.

That is certainly how it was for Schlegel each day he jogged the seven-mile trip on his way to another session with the Gorillas. And just to make sure Schlegel was suffering enough,

Gehrmann would drive past him on his way to the gym in his maroon Volkswagen Bug with black fenders and honk an ooga horn. Just as Schlegel thought Gehrmann was about to pick him up, Gehrmann would wave, smile, and keep driving.

That jog was the appetizer to a balanced meal of hardships: squats, bench presses, lifts, every rigor to which Gehrmann subjected his football players. It was those same football players who helped Schlegel survive the difficult hours he spent in their zoo, those same students of Gehrmann's who swarmed around Schlegel, nearly young enough to be his children, shouting him through that final rep, that one last squat, the extra bench press that would afflict him the next day with a body so sore as to test his willingness to keep coming back.

But Gehrmann was not just helping Schlegel. Schlegel may not have known it, but he also was helping Gehrmann. As Gehrmann's Gorillas swarmed around Schlegel to push him through a final rep, they also swarmed around the vision of what Gehrmann told them—that if the dreams they chased meant anything to them at all, then whatever they had to do to attain them would have to be hard, it would have to hurt, it would have to confront the limits of all they thought they could endure.

Gehrmann had plastered his gym with an array of signs bearing messages to his Gorillas. "If it's to be, it's up to me," one said. "Am I better today than I was yesterday?" another asked. Gehrmann believed it was important to present the kids with a positive image of themselves, and what more positive image of themselves could they encounter than that of a man such as Schlegel who had spent the lion's share of his life pursuing the right to call himself a champion?

Schlegel's favorite sign in Gehrmann's gym was one that read, "The road to success is always under construction."

To Schlegel, Gehrmann's zoo was a lot like what it was to any of his other students—not a destination, but a means of getting there. Schlegel's situation differed in at least one regard: It was not his life that awaited him the day he left Gehrmann's gym. At thirty-six years old, life was now. For Schlegel, Gehrmann's gym was a stopping-off place between a dream and its realization, between potential and actuality, between struggle and its reward.

It was the hunger for that reward that took Schlegel down four waist sizes in those grueling summer days among the Gorillas. By the time Gehrmann released Schlegel from his zoo to try his luck on tour, Schlegel was 155 pounds at 5'10" with a size 29 waist. And all those endless runs through the hilly streets of Vancouver had turned his legs as taut as two torpedoes. He wasn't going to pull a hammy this time around. He was running a six-minute mile.

Schlegel wanted to be the guy who still had something left fifty games into a tournament while others languished with exhaustion. He wanted to be the guy whose physical conditioning allowed him more easily to summon the skills any player needed to flourish on tour—speed, control, accuracy, mental toughness, an immunity to the distractions that fear and doubt imposed. If he could not beat them with the talent he had, he could beat them with the body he had built. It was a body that would not let him down in the later stretches of tournaments, and especially not on the TV show. Bowling may be stereotyped as the province of beer-bellied, blue-collar workers who otherwise spend their free time on their sofas, but the truth is that professional bowling as much demands athleticism, conditioning, and discipline as any other pro sport.

The results of Schlegel's stint with the Gorillas of Vancouver were immediate. Just weeks removed from his days in Gehrmann's zoo, at the first tournament of the 1979 season—the

Miller High Life Classic in Anaheim—Schlegel qualified for the TV show. He finished fourth. The next week, he did it once again, making the show at the Showboat Invitational in Las Vegas and cashing a fifth-place check.

Four weeks later, at the Dutch Masters Open in Detroit, he made his third TV appearance of the season. If his bowling that week spoke loudly enough of the work he had done back home, his words spoke even more loudly. ABC's Al Michaels, who was working the show as the play-by-play man, inquired about Schlegel's desire to replace his motorhome with a full-blown bus in a pre-show interview. The winner would receive $12,000. Schlegel fully expected to take every last penny of it in Detroit that day.

"Schlegel travels around in a motor home, as most of the pros do. But he wants to buy a bus and reconvert it," Michaels observed on the show. "It'll cost him $100,000. He said 'I'll pick up the twelve grand here today, there's the down payment.' So he's confident," Michaels concluded through partner Bo Burton's laughter in the booth.

About a year before Al Michaels asked America if they believed in miracles, he had stepped onto that set at Sunnybrook Lanes in Detroit and opened ABC's telecast of the PBA Dutch Masters Open with a note of amazement: A line of people circled the building in subzero temperatures that February morning to claim a seat at a pro bowling show that would not begin for another eight hours.

A top bowling pro in 1979 made $80,000—a significant amount of money—and its tour stops drew a significant crowds throughout the country. The people in the crowd had seen the first athlete in history to sign a $1 million endorsement deal in 1964: a pro bowler by the name of Don Carter. They were the days, too, when pro bowlers enjoyed a celebrity reserved for those who had attained the heights of stardom.

By 1979, enough people watched PBA telecasts on ABC each week that pro bowlers ran a genuine risk of getting pegged for an autograph while tossing a gallon of milk into their carts at the grocery store.

The scene at Sunnybrook that frigid day in Detroit confirmed the cultural prominence the sport of bowling enjoyed in America at the time. It was a time when fans crowded the row behind the TV lanes in pressed suits with flowers pinned to their lapels, the ladies among them were dressed well enough to join a wedding party after the show, and ABC sent in the big guns to call the strikes and spares—announcers such as Al Michaels, Pat Summerall, Verne Lundquist.

When Schlegel went out for a jog the morning of the show, as he now did every day, his watch froze.

"Holy shit!" he said aloud as he realized his watch read almost the same time it did when he started his jog. "I know I have been running for a while. It can't be."

Then he realized he had no idea what time it was, and that he might be late for the TV show. He made a frenzied dash back to the bowling alley, where he found Cathy screaming "Hurry! Hurry! Where the hell have you been?" Schlegel ran back to the bowling alley so fast, in fact, that he covered a mile in fewer than six minutes. To brave the Detroit cold that morning, Schlegel covered his lips and chin in Vaseline and strapped on a face mask that had lapels to attach it to his coat. The mask, too, had frozen so solid it felt like a slab of ice.

Schlegel, a masked wild man running faster than the wind with a glaze of Vaseline frosting his face like a donut, later summed up the experience with five words that rang truer that morning than ever before.

"There ain't nothing like running," he said.

There also ain't nothing like winning, and by the time he threw his final shot in Sterling Heights that afternoon, Schlegel planned to know that first hand. He threw two straight strikes to open the match and celebrated with a fist pump and gritted teeth.

A mouse-gray pair of bell-bottom slacks clung to Schlegel's taut legs so tightly they might as well have been made of Saran Wrap. A half-melon of hair curtained his clammy forehead under the sizzling lights of the TV cameras, and his bowling shoes glistened a sparkling shade of gold. Ernie Schlegel understood that fashion was a form of entertainment, and people watched the PBA tour to see a great show.

"That's what the game is all about," Schlegel would say. "It's like a boxing match. People don't want to watch a bunch of stiffs bowl."

The PBA's overlords at the time—Joe Antenora and Frank Esposito—made no room for visionaries on the PBA tour. You showed up in polyester slacks and wooden hair or you paid a fine on your way out the door. Antenora and Esposito knew only the world where people showed up for bowling tournaments dressed like maître d's. Had they allowed Schlegel to have his way, he would have been wearing velvet tuxedos and silver lamé jump suits whenever he made it onto the TV show. When the bosses got wind of Schlegel's planned regalia, they told him to show up dressed like everybody else or not bother showing up at all. They had had enough of the Bicentennial Kid; that episode tested the limits of their tolerance.

They would learn that in Schlegel's world no one tells him what to do—that inside, Schlegel was still the brash kid from the streets of New York who once fashioned a neck tie out of licorice and ate it in front of his teacher in defiance of school dress code. And it was *that* Ernie Schlegel, incensed by the PBA's assumption that it had the authority to tell him what to wear on television, who put in a phone call to PBA Commissioner Joe Antenora to suggest that he wear a tuxedo instead. It was the first of many thinly veiled "fuck you" phone calls Schlegel would issue to the PBA over his long career.

The fact remained that nothing could remove from Esposito's mind the smudge of cigarette ash in the new carpet of his Jersey bowling center years earlier, the laughing and foul-mouthed crew of kids responsible for it, their association with the man whom Esposito subsequently kicked out and banished from the PBA for years thereafter—Ernie Schlegel. Esposito may have opened the gate to Schlegel's dreams since then, but that did not mean he had to like the guy. Schlegel could not turn back time to change the events of that fateful night back in Jersey or the lost years he endured in its aftermath, and he was powerless to stop Esposito from being just as tyrannical as he pleased now.

Schlegel tried in 1978, when he threatened to pull out of a TV show he was set to bowl at a tournament in Kissimmee, Florida. Esposito told him he could not wear his lamé jump suit, a getup for which he had paid $250. So Schlegel told Esposito to go fuck himself. Then he decided he would pull out of the show altogether. Upon further reflection, he thought he would still show up to bowl and wear costume anyway. What were they going to do about it? John Mazzio, a former IBM employee from Chicago and now an Alcoholics' Anonymous counselor whom Schlegel had brought on as his "mental game advisor," tried to talk some sense into him.

"No, I don't give a fuck!" Schlegel told him. "That's what I am wearing!"

Then Cathy talked to him, and ultimately Schlegel bowled the show dressed in the plainer attire Antenora and Esposito preferred. To Schlegel, his clothes were everything; they were his incentive to shine on the show. To Schlegel, removing the costumes from his act felt like removing a champion golfer's favorite club from his bag at Augusta. Even though Schlegel relented in Kissimmee, Esposito and friends held the incident against him anyway.

Another way they cramped Schlegel's style was by timing his approach and fining him if he took longer to throw a shot than they preferred. Schlegel was so notorious for the slow pace at which he bowled that some called him "the human rain delay." One writer joked that Schlegel's approach "probably could be timed by sundial." Funny or not, that was the only way he knew how to do it. Forced to quicken his pace, he was not the bowler he needed to be. So Harry Golden, the PBA Tournament director who worked under Antenora and Esposito, started busting out a stopwatch whenever Schlegel bowled on television, tapping him on the shoulder between frames to hurry him up as he tried to focus on games worth tens of thousands of dollars. Golden's militant enforcement of the PBA's slow bowling rule—which allowed bowlers 15 seconds to make a shot once they stepped onto the approach—was dubbed "The Great Stopwatch Controversy." The rule forced Schlegel into the uncomfortable situation of having to bowl while always looking over his shoulder, waiting to be told he was taking too long. And every time he took too long for Golden's liking, Golden charged Schlegel a fine.

Esposito and friends may have banished flamboyance in favor of wool slacks and wooden smiles, but the hip pants and golden shoes Schlegel sported on the 1979 Dutch Masters Open show—a subtle echo of the man once known as the Bicentennial Kid—proved that they could never banish soul.

Schlegel's opponent, Bill Coleman, opened the game with a strike of his own, pounded the pocket for another, and then another in the third frame when his ball crossed over to the wrong side of the headpin but put all ten pins in the pit once again. A 6'2" 205-pounder out of Eugene, Oregon, Coleman looked like someone put a man's clothes on a bull. He had a rib cage built like a two-car garage and legs as thick as trees. A faintly blond mustache bushed his upper lip, and his broad forehead and balding pate shone under the television lights. His several rings glittered each time he took his ball from the rack to set up for his next shot.

Coleman had at least one advantage over Schlegel: a lone PBA title. He understood how to win in a way that Schlegel did not. And thus he had that edge of confidence Schlegel, for all his clothes and flamboyance, still lacked.

Schlegel responded with two more perfect strikes as they began the match with a combined seven consecutive strikes between them. Again, he paused at the foul line to accentuate his latest double—a vaguely frothy gritting of the teeth, a fist pump more ferocious than the last. Just as it was back at Central, it was all about the hustle here in Detroit.

Schlegel was hardly the only opponent Bill Coleman faced each time he stepped up to the approach. In Schlegel, Coleman faced all the hustlers from the Manhattan of Schlegel's youth whose legends endured in his scowls and fist pumps, the Kenny Barbers and Richie Hornreichs whose thousand-dollar matches in the middle of the night were as tough as any match he would have on tour. They were the men who long ago taught Schlegel that a scowl was worth as much as any score if it became the thing his opponent thought about, that the opponent's mind was a room he could ransack as long as he tried the right key.

Coleman stepped up in the eighth frame to demonstrate with another explosive strike that the only thing he planned to think about was beating Ernie Schlegel.

"We're dead even through eight!" Michaels shouted.

"Al, as we expected, tremendous scoring and tremendous competition," Burton said.

Coleman struck yet again for four strikes in a row, or what pro bowlers call a "four-bagger."

That was when another opponent stepped in: Schlegel's wife Cathy, who lunged from her seat and shouted after Schlegel returned Coleman's strike with a clutch strike of his own in the ninth frame, a crucial moment known as the "foundation frame" for its importance as the foundation of the final frame of the game.

A pair of 1970s shades with lenses as wide as wall clocks obscured her rouged face. Cranberry-red lipstick stunned her powdery complexion with a flourish of color as fiery as the outburst with which she celebrated Schlegel's strike. She tossed thick waves of red hair back behind her shoulders and took several emphatic breaths as she leered out from under her brow, fuming somewhere inside herself. She glared out of the corners of her eyes to see if anyone had a problem with it, perfectly prepared to give them some problems of their own if they did. Then she gathered her composure again, pulling in the sides of her coat and adjusting her seat.

Any wife of a PBA pro knows that no pressure their husbands feel on the lanes compares to the agony with which a wife endures moments like these. Schlegel was the one with the ball in his hands, but Cathy could only watch and hope.

Detroit was the hometown of the man Schlegel had to beat in a Friday-night "position round" match to make it into the Dutch Masters Open show the following day: Bob Strampe, Hall of Famer, one of a very few men to bowl a perfect game in each of five decades. Strampe was a man whose prime was long behind him, but his will to win was beyond the power of age to diminish. Sunnybrook Lanes was Strampe's home bowling alley. The locals loved him like a hero. That match was the moment Cathy became what Schlegel would later describe as "a raving lunatic."

As Schlegel and Strampe were led from the locker room to the lanes for that match, Strampe got some hometown love from the fans. They chanted "Strampe! Strampe! Strampe!"

Cathy, nervous and shaking with a desire to see her husband on the show, decided she would start a chant of her own. *The hell with this!* she thought. She leapt on top of a table, cupped her hands around her mouth, and screamed into the Strampe-loving din.

"Schleee-GEL! Schleee-GEL! Schleee-GEL!" she shouted.

Strampe laughed, and that crack in the legend's composure was exactly the advantage Schlegel was looking for. He crushed Strampe to make it onto the TV show.

"There's Schlegel's wife Cathy, and she's sure excited," Burton chuckled as Cathy exploded out of her seat on the show.

Burton, who had surely been there to see her scream Schlegel's name from a table top the day before, knew as well as anyone just how "excited" Cathy got.

As Schlegel stepped up to bowl the final frame of his match against Coleman, maybe he heard those kids in Gerhmann's gym crowd around him once again to cheer him through this latest test. Maybe he heard Gehrmann himself telling them about the things a champion does when he is down. Maybe he heard nothing but the silence of his own focused mind.

Schlegel was finishing first, Coleman last. If he threw three strikes he would force Coleman to do the same. Anything less and all Schlegel could do when he was done was sit and hope while Coleman bowled.

Here he was again, staring down sixty feet of wood at the only obstacle between himself and the champion he had planned to become that day he made his first seven-mile jog from home to Gehrmann's zoo. Just like he did against Curt Schmidt in Baltimore. Just like he did against Steve Wallace in Buffalo. Just like he had done so many times before. But he never made it out of any of those shows a winner. How many more chances would he get to win? How many chances does a professional bowler—anyone—get in a lifetime? More of those questions Schlegel could not answer.

It felt like an eternity passed before Schlegel even looked up at the pins. This time he would bowl on his own terms, fine and all, shot clock be damned. If this was one of those chances he would give away and wonder for the rest of his life where it went wrong, he would be damned before he'd give it away to Harry Golden and the stopwatch police.

The crowd erupted the second Schlegel let the shot go. Schlegel collapsed as he watched the shot, sliding across the approach on his knees. It was a beautiful shot destined for the pocket, and destined, too, to silence that word on tour that he choked in big matches. And that was when he heard them again, those superlatives that stung with their praise, the failure cloaked in compliments from those who knew how many times he had thrown this shot before, how many times he returned to his seat making plans for next week.

"And what a bad break!" Burton insisted. "A tremendously well-controlled shot by Schlegel. When he's gotten in this position before, he has usually gone high. But this time he stayed down . . . really a super, super shot with all that pressure."

The ball pounded the pocket like every previous shot he had thrown in the match, and like several shots before that did not strike, he left the right-hander's nemesis pin, the dreaded 10 pin in the corner that so often stands even on the best shots. For all the things within Schlegel's control—the curls and squats in Gehrmann's gym, the pre-show jogs where game plans swarmed his mind like bees—the standing 10 pin in the sport of bowling proves that destiny is beyond the power of any human being to govern.

No one in Sunnybrook Lanes could know it yet, but the match ended the minute Schlegel rose from his knees, flailing his arms in fury at the single pin standing between himself and his dreams.

Mathematically, it still was possible for Schlegel to emerge the winner. In fact, it even was possible for the match to culminate in a tie. But there would be no ties that afternoon, no chances to come back a second time.

Schlegel left another 10 pin on his next shot, which also crushed the pocket to no avail. In fact, every time Schlegel threw a ball he put it right where it needed to be to strike, slamming the pocket each frame, only to leave Schlegel staring at a 10 pin just once too often to win. That was how the dice of destiny rolled.

"A bit discouraged, Ernie Schlegel. That's the finest game he's ever bowled on national television," Burton said. "He's gonna go home in defeat with a 246."

Burton, himself a PBA titlist many times over, knew that no shot was "super" that left you a loser. The only thing that kept you out on tour was a wish to erase your name from the list of "great" non-champions. Not when your resentment of that foil crown was so great it compelled your wife to leap onto a tabletop and shout the name of the man who wore it as if she could scream it off of his head. Not when you had chased a dream for ten years and had only this image of yourself crumbling to the ground on national TV to show for it. Soon, the reward Schlegel and his wife pursued from town to town in their motorhome would come to them.

7

SHRUGGING OFF THE MONKEY

By 1980, Schlegel was still waiting for the elevator in the lobby of his dreams. Nelson Burton Jr. already occupied the penthouse on the top floor. Burton would enter the Hall of Fame in a year's time. He claimed his first PBA title in 1964 at age 22 and made six shows that year alone. Schlegel, meanwhile, had spent the early '60s nursing the bitter blow of his banishment from the PBA, falling asleep behind the counter of the watch store his mother worked in, loading soda trucks in the muggy heat of a New York City summer, or repairing AC units in Hackensack.

In his school days, Burton was the kind of kid who captained the baseball team to a city championship, the high school wrestler and all-around jock who made girls blush in the hallway. He went on to fly his own private Cessna from tour stop to tour stop, make news when he flew it down to the Florida Keys and yanked a 190-pound tarpon out of the sea, and win several majors on tour before Schlegel had won at all.

Bowling fans knew him as "Bo." He was the man whom broadcasting pioneer Roone Arledge—creator of Monday Night Football and Wide World of Sports—had tapped to do color commentary alongside Chris Schenkel for PBA telecasts on ABC. But he still bowled tour stops when he felt like it, and occasionally someone had to fill in for him in the broadcast booth because he still bowled his way onto the TV show now and then. As professional bowling's popularity waned in the years to come, Burton's name would become symbolic of the sport's golden era—a time when millions of viewers tuned in to watch Burton and Schenkel call the strikes and spares each Saturday on ABC.

To the action bowlers who crossed paths with him back in the early 1960s, Burton's name was symbolic of only one thing: losing your money. He showed up unannounced and unknown one night in 1961 at a place in Chicago called Miami Lanes. Most locals swore the place was run by mobsters, and everybody swore it housed some of the greatest action bowlers in the country. That was the curious thing about Burton: Many bowling alleys claimed to have the country's greatest action bowlers until he showed up to adjust their definition of "great." He had one such adjustment in store this night in Chicago.

"I have a young man here who says he will bowl anybody in the house," the manager said on the PA system. Johnny Campbell, then a local action player of modest notoriety, found that rather unusual.

Anyone who is going to come in here and make a statement like that has some real balls, he thought to himself.

A dark-haired, nineteen-year-old Burton emerged in a crew cut and a button-down white shirt and dark slacks. He looked like a polished kid reporting to the office for his first day of work. Then he started bowling. After trouncing his opponent for six straight games, Campbell, who was keeping score, realized Burton may have looked like a kid, but he bowled as well as any grown man. Burton did not bowl a single game under 240. Then Campbell wrote down his name—Nelson Burton Jr.—and it hit him.

"Oh, my God!" Campbell said. "This is Nelson Burton's son!"

Burton's father, Nelson Burton Sr., was one of the greatest bowlers in the history of the sport. And so, it seemed, was his kid.

Nearly twenty years later, when Burton Jr.'s path crossed Schlegel's at King Louie Lanes in Kansas City for the 1980 King Louie Open title match on TV, he had fifteen titles to Schlegel's zero. His last one had come weeks prior at the Fair Lanes Open in Baltimore. As a commentator, his made-for-TV tan, full head of bushy, black hair and sculpted biceps bulging in the arms of his ABC Sports coat established him as the media darling one writer called "the PBA's answer to Robert Goulet," referring to the actor who scored a breakout role as Lancelot in the Broadway musical *Camelot*.

Yes, by this point in his career, Burton was bowling royalty. How fitting, then, that he was bowling the finals of an event called the "King Louie Open" in a pair of golden bowling shoes with his cocky strut and square jaw. A beltless pair of pressed, beige slacks was buttoned up over his navel. The sleeves of his red-and-black striped polo shirt with a cotton-white collar tightened around his biceps every time he lifted his ball for another shot. The shirt clung tightly to his sculpted abdomen. With his slender legs and chiseled arms, he cut the figure of a trained athlete in a sport more commonly perceived as the refuge of beer-bellied hustlers and degenerates.

While Schlegel got in his practice shots during the commercial break, Burton talked baseball with fans in the front row as if to make sure they saw he was not sweating this, that he had been here before and come up a winner fifteen times more than Schlegel had, and he knew it.

"This is going to be a match of psyching," play-by-play man Chris Schenkel said as the match began, "because Ernie Schlegel, the tournament leader, is just full of that type of 'action,' and Bo Burton is not a slouch, either."

"Not a slouch" indeed. The Burton whom Schenkel spoke of picked up blackjack and poker at the ripe age of six. His father gave him an itch for action so fierce that the nuns he had for schoolteachers prized his penchant for numbers as if it were a divine math miracle. The nuns did not know the unsavory source of his propensity for arithmetic: learning when to hit or when to stay in a game of blackjack. That taught Burton more about numbers than any nun's math ever would.

Bowling was the one hand of cards he knew would never fail him. Not that night in Chicago, not the time he shot up his thumb with Novocaine to bowl a tour stop after thirty-eight games of action the night before, not the time he was stripped of his stripes as an Army Sergeant for reporting to duty late after another long night on the lanes.

"They tossed me in the guardhouse for twenty-four hours, and I went back to private for a while," he remembered years later. "I didn't mind much, because I figured I had made the equivalent of a year's pay in those matches."

Burton's days of banging heads with bowlers in the mob haunts of Chicago were the memories of another man's life by 1980. With a cushy TV gig that paid in one year what he used to make in one good night on the lanes, the checks he bowled for amounted to little more than beer money. Burton never again would depend on his ball and shoes to pay the bills, but money is not the thing that feeds the ego of a born competitor. Only winning does that, and then the next win, and the next. When Burton looked across the ball return and shook hands with Schlegel to start the final match of the King Louie Open, he did not see a man or a fellow bowler. He saw his next win.

Schlegel's raiment struck a balance between Frank Esposito's dated taste and Schlegel's urge to dazzle. He tucked a steel-gray, V-neck shirt into a beltless pair of violet slacks whose bottoms roiled around his ankles as he shuffled toward the foul line. He wore a yolk-colored baseball glove under the blue Dick Weber wrist support most bowlers Velcroed around their wrist on TV to rake in some endorsement dough. His thick bush of bowl-cut, dirty blonde hair looked like someone halved a pumpkin, painted it the color of honey, and plopped it on top of his head.

The packed crowd behind the lanes erupted with exclamations of "Come on, Ernie!" as he glided into his first shot and blasted the pocket. It was a strike, the first of many he would throw that afternoon.

Cathy sported an emerald silk, emerald shirt in the crowd, her pale cheeks stunned with a subtle flourish of rouge. A shock of permed, auburn bangs obscured her forehead and hovered over her wide-lens glasses. Beside her sat Sy Marks, a buddy of Schlegel's from the old neighborhood, with a trimmed, dark goatee and a sharkskin suit. To the Schlegels, Sy's presence made everything feel like yesterday.

"There, you see he's five-eleven, one-fifty-five, and can you *believe* it? He's looking for his first title," Schenkel said as Schlegel's stats appeared on screen. The stats documented the twelve years he had spent on tour, the quarter-of-a-million dollars in earnings he had bagged over that time, the goose egg where his number of PBA titles ought to have been.

"It's very hard for our pro members to believe that he is looking for a title for the first time," said Dick Weber, filling in for Burton, of the gaping zero, "because he is an excellent bowler."

Weber calling you an excellent bowler was like Wilt Chamberlain telling you that you're a hell of a basketball player. Bowling's Mount Rushmore began with Dick Weber's face. With twenty-six PBA titles and accolades strung across nearly half a century of bowling, the man was the sport's marquee legend.

Burton greeted Schlegel's opening strike with an even more convincing one of his own. He wasted little time strutting back to the ball return with a vaguely annoyed expression on his face, as if no non-titlist had any business burdening him with the need to show up in a championship match. For the rest of the afternoon, Burton would perceive Schlegel the way he had perceived so many other challengers over the years—as a fruit fly he meant to swipe off his armor in a joust.

Burton's next shot sailed left of the headpin. A single pin remained. He sauntered back to retrieve his ball, shrugged, and sighed. He stared down the lane as if the pins had to be kidding him. His next shot sailed left again and nearly missed the spare. Burton paused at the line in disbelief. It seemed, for a moment, as if bowling's golden boy might not be so golden this time around.

It is customary for a bowler on a PBA show to stay put in his seat until the opposing player completes his shot. Schlegel had never been much for custom, and as a jolt of adrenaline coursed through his body after watching Burton nearly miss an easy spare and stiffen with embarrassment, he launched out of his seat before Burton even turned away from the foul line. There was an urgency about him, the mildly angry desperation of a man determined not to let this afternoon join the many bad memories he had made in this spot before.

Adrenaline is a fickle assistant. In moderation it may be the edge you need, but let it consume you and it can easily mean your demise. Schlegel leered at the pins with his reptilian squint, ball in hand. He rushed to the line and the ball seemed to drop from his hand as he let it go. He fell off balance to his right and watched the ball whiff the headpin and leave four pins standing.

Schlegel's next shot was a strike, but the damage was done. To miss a spare in a championship match against a bowler of Burton's pedigree was to leave a trace of blood in shark-infested waters. It was merely a matter of time before you were destroyed. Burton swaggered into position to throw his next shot, cradling his ball in his arms as he adjusted his blue and white bowling glove and holding his hand over the air blowing out of the ball return. If you did not know he was bowling for a top prize of $11,000 dollars, you might have thought he was preparing for a walk to the post office. His placid demeanor could not have struck a starker contrast to Schlegel's jittery intensity.

Burton fired his ball into the pocket, left a 10 pin standing, and converted the spare with the textbook aplomb for which he was known. When the camera honed in on Schlegel, he was crouching over the ball return and holding a knife in plain view of Burton, who was gathering himself for his next shot. Schlegel picked up his ball and took it back to his seat with his knife, the blade twice as long as his index finger, and began fidgeting with the thumb hole in his ball. No image could possibly be more emblematic of a match between the prince groomed for glory and the former gangster.

Weber attempted to explain away the sight as typical of bowlers so fraught with nerves the blood rushes out of their fingers and makes the finger holes feel bigger, a problem only another piece of thumb tape can fix.

Ostensibly, the knife helped Schlegel stuff a piece of tape into the thumb hole of his bowling ball, but if Burton happened to be thinking about Schlegel's knife when he set up for his next shot, well, call that a bonus. This may have been Kansas City, but this also was a game Schlegel picked up in the shady haunts of Brooklyn or the Bronx—a game as much of the mind as of anything else.

It was Schlegel's mind Burton was after when he stuffed his next ball into the pocket for his finest strike of the match—a shot aimed at Schlegel's gamesmanship. Burton already was walking back to his seat when the camera found him again seconds after his shot, poker-faced and unfazed. In this psychological standoff between Schlegel's knife and Burton's moxie, Burton's moxie had won. Schlegel's antics may have earned him his share of money back home, but here in Kansas City, opposite one of the greatest bowlers the tour had ever seen, he would have to win with his score alone.

Schlegel buried his next three shots for strikes, chomping furiously on a piece of gum. Burton struggled into his sixth frame—a spare here, a bad shot followed by an open frame there. The slow-motion replay captured Burton wincing and turning away from the pins with the stiff manner of a stunned man. Maybe he got away with a lousy shot now and then that long-ago night in Chicago, where Johnny Campbell noted the name of the cocky kid in the button-down shirt who never bowled a game under 240. Those were matches against men whose names no one remembered; this was a match against a man who someday would join him in the most elite club the sport has to offer—the Hall of Fame. The far-away look in Burton's eyes as he took his seat after blowing a spare betrayed the surrender of a champion who knew he was running out of time. In all likelihood, he may have already coughed up the title on the kind of spare he converted a thousand times a year.

Burton's struggles made Schlegel's next ball perhaps the most crucial shot of his life. A strike here would bring him closer to the thing he had chased across the country for more than a decade—his first PBA title. Many thoughts flashed through his mind as he stood and stared down the pins, his bowling ball ribboned with a stripe of lane oil that glistened under the TV lights. Maybe he thought about those years he spent waiting on the sidelines of his dreams, or the blow this title would deal to those who had stood between him and this moment—Harry Golden and his stopwatch, Frank Esposito and his grudges.

Schlegel took a deep, heaving breath, the sweaty edges of his bowl-cut hair clinging to his clammy forehead, and took his first step toward the foul line.

"Legs trembling now, he's moving to the line, he's yet to win," Schenkel said as Schlegel glided into his shot and let the ball go.

At first the shot looked awfully similar to the one that sailed by the headpin in the second frame—the only frame in which he did not strike. Then it meandered in the direction of the pocket from somewhere out near the gutter, making it all the way to the headpin as Schlegel pressed his fists together at the foul line and stiffened with hope. All pins cleared the deck except for the 7 pin in the corner, which withstood Schlegel's shot for a split second before another pin lunged out of the gutter and slapped it out. Strike.

When Schlegel struck yet again on his next shot, Cathy, stunning in her brilliant emerald blouse and auburn hair, exploded out of her seat. Then she swiveled to her side and swung a clenched fist down like some livid judge pounding her gavel to manage an unruly court. There were many injustices she meant to avenge with her husband's triumph this afternoon—that night screaming away a pro-Strampe crowd with shouts of her husband's name from a table top in Detroit, the tyranny of the fashion police who dulled Schlegel's edges when they forced him into the clothes of a square, the many titles she had watched slip through his fingers since their hasty wedding. All of it, if Schlegel could hang on for the win, would fade into this long-awaited triumph over the past and its many bruising failures.

With his fifth consecutive strike and sixth in seven frames, Schlegel was virtually assured of the title. It was exactly the point in the match when Burton found his shot. He rushed to the approach after Schlegel's fifth strike and tossed one of his own, so disgruntled with his own performance that he sauntered back to the ball return shaking his head. Though a 7 pin stood despite another great shot on his next ball, it would be the last time he left a pin on the deck for the rest of the game. Frame after frame Burton pounded the pocket for a strike—the ninth frame, then the first in the tenth, and the second, and the third.

There was one problem for Burton, and his name was Ernie Schlegel. Schlegel's face assumed the scowling expression of the Other Ernie as he watched his next ball crush the pocket for his sixth strike in a row. It was a look of such irascible menace that neither Weber nor Schenkel could contain their laughter at Schlegel's intensity. Schlegel swung his arms wildly through the air after blowing back all ten pins. He crouched down and clutched his fists, falling out of the camera's view and exposing, once again, an ecstatic wife who darted out of her seat and pumped her fist in the crowd.

For perhaps the first time that afternoon, viewers noticed something else about Cathy. She was clutching something in her left hand—a stuffed monkey. The monkey was a gift given to her by a business partner. She tossed it to Schlegel.

He kissed it and tossed it back to her in the crowd. At last, Schlegel had shrugged the monkey off his back. He now could call himself a PBA champion. Here, finally, was a title few action bowlers ever attained, and the conclusion of a quest that began in the smoky bowling alleys of New York City all those years ago.

8

THE LAST GREAT ACTION MATCH

One thing Schlegel liked to say throughout his career is that you're born insane; you have to work your whole life to get sane. At the 1995 Touring Players Championship, a major on the PBA Tour, Schlegel was about to make it clear that he was still working on it. At age fifty-two, fifteen years after he won his first championship, he had qualified to bowl the championship round live on ESPN. During the week's competition, he had bowled two 300 games and a 299, besting players who were young enough to be his children and who threw the ball with considerably more power and hook than Schlegel ever had. If he won, he would become the oldest player in PBA history to win a major title.

By then, Schlegel had amassed five PBA titles. After waiting twelve years to win his first one at the 1980 King Louie Open, he won his second title just 10 weeks later at the 1980 City of Roses Open in Portland, Oregon. Mount St. Helen's had just blown apart, and a layer of ash settled on the lanes. Players' bowling balls were coming back through the ball return ringed with a stripe of volcanic ash. It seemed the perfect metaphor for a career that suddenly was on fire.

Schlegel came within one ball of winning his first major the following year. He advanced to the title match of the 1981 PBA National Championship, blowing out Dave Davis 245-171, and then defeating legend Dick Weber—the same man who had announced his win the previous year—on his way to a contest with the equally legendary Earl Anthony. By 1981, Anthony, a lefty, had become an indomitable force on the PBA Tour. He already had won the PBA National Championship three times. Schlegel battled Anthony down to the final ball. Needing a strike on the first ball in the tenth frame, Schlegel's ball just never quite found its way to the pocket, leaving the 2 pin on a light hit and letting Anthony squeak his way to his fourth PBA National Championship victory, 242-237.

Schlegel again surfaced in the title matches of the 1984 Long Island Open in Garden City, New York, and the 1985 Lite Beer Open in North Olmsted, Ohio, respectively, winning them both for his third and fourth titles. He showed up on the 1984 show clad entirely in a fire-engine red outfit, complete with red pants, a red hand towel, a red bowling ball, red shoes, and a red-and-white striped shirt. Cathy called it "color therapy." The more aggressive his colors on the show, the theory went, the more aggressively he would bowl. For the 1985 show, he donned a violet top with sparkling, gold stripes strung along each side like suspenders and snow-white pants with violet-tinged bell-bottoms that roiled around his shoes as he stepped toward the foul line.

Schlegel savored that latter victory in particular. At the time, the tour featured a triumvirate of tournaments collectively called the "Lite Slam." They included the Lite Beer Classic in Miami, the Lite Beer Open, and the Lite Beer Championship in Milwaukee. If the same bowler won all three Lite Beer events, that bowler would win $1 million. Pete Weber had won the first, and made it to the title match of the second. Had he defeated Schlegel, just one more event stood between himself and the jackpot. Schlegel would rather have been crushed by a truck in the street than allow somebody to walk over him on his way to becoming a millionaire.

In 1989, at the Arc Pinole Open in Pinole, California, the lights went out in the bowling alley due to an electrical failure halfway through Schlegel's semifinal match against Ron Williams. Williams sat through most of the 17-minute delay, while Schlegel earned chuckles and strange looks from spectators by jogging in place on the set. Williams promptly missed a spare coming out of the delay, and Schlegel seized the momentum with two strikes in a row en route to victory. Williams struck out to shoot 254, but Schlegel, too, pounded the pocket the rest of the game for a 258. He then clobbered Dave D'Entremont in the title match, 268-215.

Then the lights went out somewhere else—this time, they went dark in Schlegel's bowling career. With the exception of the 1993 Masters, where he qualified for the TV show but lost his only match, he failed to make an appearance on a single TV show in the five years following his 1989 Arc Pinole Open victory. His appearance in the championship round of the 1995 Touring Players Championship at age fifty-two, then, was nothing short of stunning. The show would take place before a sold-out crowd at Pittsburgh's Robert Morris College Sewall Center arena, where bowling lanes had been specially constructed for the event. An arena full of screaming fans was exactly the kind of setting in which Schlegel felt he was born to perform.

One thing few people in that arena or watching at home knew was that Schlegel had someone other than himself or his wife of twenty years to bowl for—someone who could watch only from a hospital bed.

In 1976, Schlegel and Cathy met John Mazzio in a diner up the block called The Dog House. The name of the place was particularly appropriate; Schlegel had just concluded a miserable round in a PBA tournament. Mazzio was a former IBM employee out of Chicago who more recently had become an Alcoholics' Anonymous counselor. He also happened to be a fair bowler himself, and he had a way with psychology. It was Mazzio who would complete a stage in Schlegel's self-improvement project that even Gehrmann could not address: controlling the Other Ernie. The Other Ernie was the person who pulled a knife on Mike Ginsberg, and the one whom Jerry Markey spotted outside of a Boy Scouts meeting trying to shoot a kid in the face with his zip gun over a petty slight. The Other Ernie was dangerous; he was a part of him that Schlegel did not like. Mazzio knew Schlegel needed help finding a way to run from that piece of himself.

Mazzio's penchant for psychology enabled him to tinker with the crossed wires of Schlegel's mind and see what might come of it. The bizarre prescriptions he concocted proved to be the remedy Schlegel needed. They included, among other things, beating motel beds with a tennis racket in a screaming rage between rounds on tour. A terrified Cathy waited it out in the next room while her husband went berserk.

Schlegel almost always bowled better in the round following a rage session. Here was a way of relieving tension that Schlegel understood. Beating things, screaming—Schlegel knew how to do that. Mazzio would take Schlegel on mile-long walks, talking the whole time, nudging him to quit smoking and smudge the Other Ernie out of his soul. All Schlegel needed, it turned out, was a generous supply of tennis rackets, a motel bed sturdy enough to take the beating, and some honest self-analysis.

As people watched this "greatest non-champion" embark on a sensational season under Mazzio's guidance in 1976, one filled with telecast appearances and a fattening wallet to show for it, Mazzio soon acquired some monikers of his own. Bowling magazines called him "The Exorcist," "Shrink to the Stars," "a gestalt therapist." One published an illustration depicting Schlegel with a necklace of skulls, a horned mask, and a crow's head clutched in his fist.

By 1984, Schlegel told one journalist, "I'm forty-one years old now, and I'm no longer a raving lunatic."

Now, on the eve of the 1995 Touring Players Championship, Mazzio was in the hospital suffering from late-stage heart disease.

Schlegel and Cathy, devoted vegetarians, both knew of the history of stroke and diabetes in Mazzio's family. Mazzio figured he knew one ailment or the other would be his demise, but fate had a third possibility in mind—the heart attack from which he had suffered months earlier. Mazzio shared his doctor's admonishments with Cathy over dinner not long after that—the exercise he was not getting, the foods he should not be eating, the life he may not be living much longer. Then he promptly ordered a large steak. Cathy saw no point in preaching the gospel of vegetarianism. Mazzio, the sidekick with whom Schlegel and Cathy had created so many memories traveling the country together on tour over the years, would go out his way.

Mazzio's health problems had diminished his influence in Schlegel's life by then, and that fellow known as the Other Ernie started showing his face more often. Only Mazzio had managed to quell the menace Schlegel contained within himself and without his constant presence, Schlegel found himself once again resorting to the less savory means of conflict resolution he had practiced on Ginsberg back at Manhattan Lanes.

Back home at a bowling alley earlier that year, management informed him of their decision to halt their longstanding policy of allowing him to practice for free as their "house pro." Schlegel was none too pleased, and he let them know about it. Then he left. But his godsons persuaded him to return to the establishment weeks later, when a young, local bowler, sitting nearby in the company of some girls he wished to impress at Schlegel's expense, quipped about a distinction between pros and has-beens. He asserted that Schlegel fell squarely in the latter camp. Schlegel told the local it was funny that he had anything to say about either pros or has-beens, since he was not good enough to be either one.

The guy followed Schlegel into the restroom. Out of the corner of his eye, Schlegel saw the guy coming at him from behind and stepped aside. Schlegel slammed him up against the wall and jammed his thumbs into his eyes. Then he made a request.

"Tell me when your eyeballs hit your fucking brain," he said.

Schlegel pressed his thumbs into the guy's skull as he screamed in pain.

Then some things occurred to him, things he never thought of before Mazzio came around. Things like consequences. Like the possibility that the reason this tough guy provoked Schlegel into a fight was to have a reason to sue him. Things like Schlegel's fear that he might kill the poor bastard, as he had come within inches of doing to Ginsberg. Jail was not exactly the kind of place where he wished to spend his retirement. So he let the guy go and turned toward the urinal. All he wanted to do, after all, was take a piss in peace. The local was not about to walk away with those girls waiting on the other side knowing he had gotten his ass kicked by a fifty-two-year-old man. So he snuck up behind Schlegel and smashed him into the wall, cracking one of Schlegel's ribs. The two fell to the floor, and Schlegel displayed the knife he always carried on him in case some stupid bastard coaxed the Other Ernie out of his dormancy. He had such a stupid bastard on his hands now.

"I've got a knife in my hand, and I am going to count three seconds," Schlegel told him. The guy got off of him and left.

At the Sewell Center arena in Pittsburgh months later, Schlegel knew he may not get another chance to win one for Mazzio. Schlegel and his wife may have been the only two people in the world who believed he still had another title in him. Making the show at his age was itself a feat to behold. Winning the tournament outright? That would be too much to believe. The fact that a victory would make him the oldest player in PBA history to win a major was testimony to its unlikelihood.

Those were the thoughts on Schlegel's mind at the Touring Players Championship in Pittsburgh that night. With history to be made and $40,000 on the line—which would be the largest single paycheck of his professional bowling career—there were many more thoughts he wished to plant in the minds of his opponents. He wanted them to memorize the scowl gashed across his face as he burst down the aisle of the packed and frenzied auditorium to be introduced to the crowd. He wanted them to understand why the announcer labeled him professional bowling's "Iron Man," the bowler who held the record for most PBA tournaments bowled at 741.

When he stepped up to the approach to make his first televised shot in years, many Schlegels stood there with him—some he did not want to know, others he knew too well, and all of them inescapable. The Schlegel who cradled his best buddy in his arms on the roof of an apartment building in upper Manhattan, watching him die of the same heroin overdose that robbed his youth of so many friends; the Schlegel who shoved the blade of a belly-puncher in Mike Ginsberg's chest outside Manhattan Lanes; the Schlegel who showed up with an overnight bag for an unannounced stay at the house of the woman he had just met, fully intending to propose to her. The Ernie Schlegel who was about to entertain a sold-out arena in Pittsburgh was many men whose lives he had lived and never left behind. They were angels and killers, lovers and madmen, salesmen and suckers. None of them, though, was a loser.

In the twilight of a career nearly everyone presumed dead, with the hot lights of TV cameras oiling his face just as they did at his first TV appearance so many years ago, Schlegel was still up to his old action tricks. He wore a Breathe-Right strip across the bridge of his gnarled nose, a thick pair of wide-lens glasses over his squinty eyes, and the slender build he maintained over the years. He looked more like a substitute teacher in your kid's chemistry class than the flashy comic book character with the strawberry-blond bangs he called the Bicentennial Kid in younger days. It was hardly the image of a man to be feared—exactly the kind of disarming facade he discovered in a ruffled sleeve or a whiff of bourbon so long ago.

The golden days of action bowling were long-dead by 1995, but the most eccentric and incorrigible character of the action bowling era—Ernie Schlegel—was still very much alive and well. The screaming fans who filled the Sewall Center were about to reawaken his action bowling instincts. His opponent, Randy Pedersen, was younger than Schlegel by nearly twenty years. Though Pedersen did not know it yet, ESPN was about to bring the peculiar spectacle of action bowling a prominence it had never previously enjoyed. And it would do so at his expense.

The first obstacle Schlegel faced had nothing to do with the opponent he would bowl on the show. It had to do with the lanes themselves. The specially constructed lanes installed in the arena presented a completely different playing environment than the one the finalists faced in competition throughout the week. They had bowled the tournament in a traditional, bowling alley setting at a place called Olympic Lanes in Harmarville, Pennsylvania; now the finalists would have to bowl on a completely different lane surface. What worked for them at Olympic Lanes would not necessarily work for them now. These lanes had significantly less wear on them, having been bowled on a lot less frequently than the lanes in a bowling alley that hosted leagues nearly every night of the week and recreational bowling in the meantime. Schlegel, like all other competitors on the show, probably would have to find a different way of attacking the lanes than he had used as he battled his way into the championship round.

Even today, before every PBA telecast, the finalists are allowed a practice session in which they try different bowling balls, different angles to the pocket, different hand positions to make the ball react in certain ways as it rolls down the lane. The practice session is an opportunity for the players to acquaint themselves with what is called the "oil pattern," which refers to the volume and distribution pattern of oil that has been applied to the lane.

Lane oil was originally used as a protective coating to help the lanes endure the pummeling they take game after game. Resurfacing or replacing lanes is a great expense to proprietors—an expense they seek to avoid to protect their bottom line. But in the modern era of the sport, lane oil, like a bunker on a golf course, is used to vary the difficulty of the game. Some lane patterns, due to the volume of oil used and where on the lane it is applied, are particularly challenging; others make the game so easy they practically guide the ball toward the pocket. Some lane patterns are particularly slick or long, which makes it difficult for the ball to curve or hook toward the pocket. Other patterns feature less volume or a shorter length of oil, thereby increasing the amount of friction between the bowling ball and the surface of the lane and making the ball curve or hook much more aggressively.

Schlegel was known for throwing the ball much straighter than other players, relying more on his accuracy than on his ability to hook the ball across the lane to create an extreme angle into the pocket. Very slick lane conditions put him at a significant disadvantage. More powerful players who throw the ball with a lot of hook can overcome the lane pattern, whereas a straighter player like Schlegel struggles to get his ball to the headpin. The players who get lined up in practice—meaning they find a combination of the right bowling ball and the right angle down the lane to consistently strike—are usually the ones who perform well when the show goes to air. The ones who struggle to find a shot they like typically struggle on the show and lose. In the practice session before the 1995 Touring Players Championship went to air, Schlegel was lost. On the specially constructed lanes installed at Sewall Center, Schlegel could not get his ball to hook. He feared he was about to make a damned fool of himself on the show. There was only one man to call: Larry Lichstein.

"Larry, I got nothin'," Schlegel complained. "I can't get a wrinkle."

Lichstein knew exactly what Schlegel meant. In the argot of professional bowling, a player who cannot get the ball to hook will sometimes complain that he "can't get a wrinkle."

Lichstein had worked as the Players Services Director for the PBA Tour for decades. After Central Lanes burned to the ground and the action bowling scene began to die down, he followed his buddies onto the PBA Tour. In 1969, he won the vaunted "Rookie of the Year" award. Two years later, he won his lone PBA title at the 1971 Ebonite Open in San Jose. Soon thereafter, he quit the tour to become the Player Services Director, busing players' bowling balls from stop to stop on a Greyhound bus he had bought used and renovated to accommodate his business.

Lichstein's business thrived; he made so much money over the years that players would joke that Lichstein was bowler of the year every year. He easily made more money drilling balls than any player on tour made throwing them. Lichstein drilled thousands of bowling balls for the players—sometimes asking only for a percentage of their winnings as payment for his services—and he soon became the sport's preeminent mad scientist. Long before the modern-day bowling balls that feature complex physics and chemistry enabling them to perform with far greater power than ever before, Lichstein was experimenting with different ways of drilling bowling balls to make them react in different ways according to a player's style or preference. He was doing with science what action bowlers did with mercury or lead sinkers back in the 1960s.

Increasingly, bowlers wanted bowling balls with more friction that would cause the ball to hook more aggressively. When Lichstein launched his business in the early 1970s, a bowler who created even a slightly more angular entry into the pocket might slap out a 10 pin on a pocket shot one more time per game than the next guy—an extra strike where a straighter player might have to settle for a spare. Over the course of a week-long tournament, such an advantage could add up to a hundred pins or more.

In 1973, a bowler named Don McCune somehow got wind of an idea that changed the game forever: If he placed his bowling ball over a bucket full of a chemical solvent called butanone (also called methyl ethyl ketone), which is much like the acetone found in nail polish remover, the solvent would soften the surface of the bowling ball. This imperceptible softening of the ball's shell—a practice called "fuming"— would increase the friction between the bowling ball and the surface of the lane, enabling the ball to "grab" the lane more aggressively and generating much more hook than a ball with a harder surface could muster. McCune did this from tour stop to tour stop, keeping the secret to himself while blasting his way to six PBA titles that season alone and ultimately grabbing Player of the Year honors. Legend has it that some of McCune's fellow players got McCune drunk one night and kept pestering him to spill the secret of his success. This was an especially relevant question in McCune's case, because McCune, like Schlegel, was known to throw one of the straightest balls on tour. How, then, was he now hooking the ball more than anyone else out there, crushing the pins with such force that some of them went flying across the pin deck as though they had been blasted by a grenade? Eventually, McCune let that purring cat out of the bag.

The trick spread across the tour like wildfire, and bowlers began filling the bathtubs and toilets in their hotel rooms with the highly flammable chemical and soaking their bowling balls overnight. Others would leave their bowling balls over buckets full of the stuff under exterior staircases around the hotel grounds. The fumes permeated the air, and there was enough solvent to blow any hotel sky-high if a spark from somebody's cigarette happened to drift toward one of the buckets. Bowling balls subjected to this method of alteration became known as "soakers," and when PBA executives caught on to the phenomenon, they swiftly banned the practice on tour.

Meanwhile, chemists at bowling ball companies also caught on and began mixing chemicals into the compounds they used to create bowling balls that essentially added "built-in hook." These balls became known as "bleeders," because they left a bit of condensation in the plastic bag the manufacturers packed them in before sealing them in a box and shipping them off to pro shops. Pros would hound pro shops from one tour stop to the next, digging through their stockpiles of balls to find the ones that had the greatest amount of condensation in their packaging. The ones with the most condensation also happened to be the ones with the softest shell—that is what the bowlers believed, at least. Pros would pay a pro shop manager $100 for a ball that normally cost $40 if its bag contained more condensation than others. The PBA once again had to step in. They began "testing" bowling balls with a device known as a durometer, which measures the softness of the bowling ball's outer shell. Balls that registered lower than 75 were banned as "too soft." Chemists at the ball manufacturing companies honed their science to produce bowling balls that struck a reading of 75 on the dot, ball after ball; their quality control eventually achieved a precision the sport had never seen before.

Yet another way to alter the surface of a bowling ball was to rub it with sandpaper. This method became particularly popular by the early 1980s, a time when the hissing sound of sandpaper striking ball surfaces throughout the bowling alley made the place sound like it was inhabited by a gigantic snake. Some bowlers would pat their bowling balls with rosin bags, small sacks of chalk-like powder that dried their hands to ensure the ball would not slip off their fingers at the release. The rosin helped the ball grab the lane more aggressively and created the hook that players were looking for—an edge that could mean the difference between a major payday and a major disappointment. This, too, soon became illegal on tour.

Later, The Brunswick Corporation released a ball called the LT-48, which was a Johnny Petraglia signature ball. It featured Petraglia's signature etched in white print. Petraglia then had become one of the tour's biggest names; in 1980, he won the coveted Triple Crown by winning the tour's triumvirate of majors—the U.S. Open, The PBA National Championship, and the Tournament of Champions. The LT-48 had crushed almond shells mixed into the ball surface, so that it would grip the lane hard right out of the box. The rough texture made sandpaper less of a necessity. Proprietors of the bowling alleys that hosted PBA Tour events became incensed. At some stops, the damage done by sanded-down balls and exotic products such as the LT-48 forced them to resurface their lanes out of pocket.

Schlegel knew these various techniques as well as Lichstein did; they both had lived it out on tour over the years. To that extent, the advice he got from Lichstein when he placed his desperate call during practice at the Touring Players Championship made some sense.

"Take the shittiest ball in your bag, one you absolutely know you will not use on the show, and sand it down until it is as white as chalk," Lichstein advised. "Then throw that one right up the first arrow for the rest of the practice session."

The first arrow was the arrow nearest to the gutter, the five board, on the extreme outside portion of the lane. Schlegel had heard of sanding the surface of a bowling ball, of course, but why would he do this to the ball he absolutely would not use on the show? What was the point of that? Lichstein had the answer; but for now all he needed Schlegel to do was shut up and listen. He told Lichstein he would do it and hung up the phone.

Schlegel had his caddy, Chris von Krueger, sand down the surface of one of his bowling balls as much as possible and hand it back to him. Then he began to throw it. The coarsening of the ball's surface made it begin to hook as soon as it touched the surface of the lane. It hooked so much, in fact, that it curved clear across the entire lane and ended up in the left-hand gutter. This happened on shot after shot. Schlegel was puzzled. What the hell was Lichstein thinking? He called Lichstein back.

"Larry, it's hooking off my hand. Every ball ends up in the left gutter. What the hell is going on?"

"Perfect," Lichstein said. "Now, just keep doing it and call me back in ten minutes."

Schlegel hung up and went back to throwing gutter balls. As the time to air drew nearer, he started getting nervous. With five minutes left to spare, he called Lichstein again.

"Larry, it's five minutes before the show and I'm still watching my ball go into the left gutter," Schlegel explained. "I have no shot."

"OK, now get the ball you know you want to use on the show, move in to the second arrow, and throw the ball straight up the boards."

Lichstein was advising that Schlegel move five boards left and throw the ball straight up the lane rather than throwing it away from the pocket and waiting for the ball to hook back, which increasingly was the way the younger players bowled. Schlegel did not realize what he had done, but Lichstein had just coached him on how to manipulate the lane condition for his own advantage. By following Lichstein's instructions, Schlegel had just created his own "track" shot, the one he coached Lemon to take advantage of back at Gun Post Lanes all those years ago. The ball he threw during the practice session had been sanded down so much that it was actually sucking the oil off the surface of the lane, creating a "dry spot" that would allow Schlegel to get that "wrinkle" he previously could not find. Schlegel unknowingly had completely altered the lane pattern to his liking. From that moment forward, the lanes were his. Schlegel knew plenty about how to manipulate the ball surface, but this was something new to him. For all he knew, no player ever done something like this before. This practice would become commonplace on tour in the years ahead. Here again, Lichstein was ahead of his time.

The four other finalists accompanying Schlegel in the practice session were Brian Himmler, David Ozio, Brian Voss, and Randy Pedersen, the top seed. In the opening match, Voss, a PBA Hall of Famer, destroyed Himmler, 264-164. In the next match, Voss bested Ozio, another PBA Hall of Famer, by a score of 280-247. Schlegel, the second seed on the show, then squeaked by Voss, 226-218. Voss needed to strike on his first ball in the tenth frame to win and move on to the title match against Pedersen. Instead, he threw an errant shot and left a split. That left Schlegel and Pedersen to battle it out for the top prize of $40,000.

Pedersen stepped up amid the din of the arena's boisterous crowd to open the game. With his sparkling smile and Hollywood looks, he cut the figure of some blond Don Johnson. Years later, as his competitive career wound down, those looks would earn him a gig as the PBA's color analyst on ESPN, a position he would hold for more than a decade. For now, he was the cocky kid from San Marino who joined the tour at age eighteen and bought a brand new Chevy Camaro Z-28 after winning his first PBA title six years later. When he cradled his ball on the approach to make his first shot, he did it with the self-assured smirk of one who had no doubt he would do today what he had always done in this spot before—take the money home. Pedersen had bowled six prior title matches from the top-seeded position in his career. He won every time.

Two wobbly pins withstood his first shot. For a second it seemed they might both remain and leave Pedersen with the disastrous prospect of a split in the opening frame. Then, somehow, they drowsily peeled away from each other and keeled over. The crowd roared. Pedersen, with his cropped blond hair stiffened with gel and his golden complexion gleaming under the lights, looked to the roof to perform the sign of the cross, shot Schlegel a sheepish look, and took his seat.

Pedersen's stroke of luck armed Schlegel with precisely the kind of psychological ammunition he needed. Here he was, a fifty-two-year-old man who had made it this far by pounding the pocket all week against kids half his age, and he had to sit through a lousy shot and a lucky break in the opening frame of a match for forty grand?

Schlegel's father always told him that whenever he felt he had been wronged, he had to fight. Those words rang as true now as ever before. Time to fight.

He crunched the pocket on his opening shot for a strike, pumped his fist, and ran across the neighboring lane shouting "Yeah! Come on!" through clenched teeth. He quickly set up for his next shot, scowling at the pins with a face contorted by rage. Then he tossed another perfect strike, turned to glower at Pedersen, and said "You're mine!" The crowd erupted.

The match, as they say, was on.

"He's saying 'You're mine.' He's talking to Randy Pedersen," Earl Anthony observed from the broadcast booth. "That's an action bowler, folks! He wants you to think about anything but your game. So he talks to you. That's Ernie!"

Anthony then was the winningest player in the history of the PBA Tour. He had won forty-three titles, one of them a major coming at Schlegel's expense in the title match of the vaunted PBA National Championship in 1981. Anthony edged out Schlegel that day by a score of 242-237. He previously had beaten Schlegel in the TV finals of the 1978 AMF Magiscore Open in Kissimmee, Florida. By 1995, they had long-since become great friends, and Cathy had become a close friend of Anthony's wife, Susan. By 1995, Anthony played more golf than he bowled, but he did provide commentary for the PBA alongside his broadcast partner and fellow PBA Hall of Famer, Mike Durbin.

As Pedersen grabbed his ball to set up for his next shot, the crowd was still cheering so loudly that Pedersen paused and retreated from the approach with ball in hand. Then he turned to the raucous fans and smiled before trying to get set again. Though only moderately better than his previous shot, this one nonetheless found its way to the pocket. The 10 pin briefly withstood the blow; then another pin rolled across the deck and knocked it back into the pit. Pedersen, sensing now that to bowl an action player for $40,000 was to be locked in a cage with an untamed animal, gave Schlegel a taste of the action he was better known for dishing out. Pedersen paused at the line, shook a clenched fist at the pins, and roared, veins popping out of his reddening neck. He walked away looking back at the lane screaming "That's right! That's what I'm talking about! Right there!"

The crowd became hysterical.

"Is Randy the type that would talk right back to him?" broadcaster Mike Durbin asked his partner in the booth.

"Randy's liable to do anything," Anthony retorted.

Durbin was himself a PBA Hall of Famer. He had won fourteen titles. In 1984, he set a record when he won the coveted Tournament of Champions title for a third time.

It seemed Pedersen was liable to do one thing in particular that day—strike. He packed the pocket in frame three for three strikes in a row. Then he gestured wildly to the roaring crowd, circling the settee area where he and Schlegel would wait out each other's shots in their seats, shouting with his tan face turning ruddy and his brow slickening with sweat under the set's hot lights.

"Tell you what, we're not a long way from downtown Pittsburgh, but I bet they can hear us in Harrisburg right now!" Anthony said of the crowd Pedersen whipped into a riot.

Schlegel stepped up and demolished the pocket yet again on his next shot, but this time he left the right-hander's nemesis: the 10 pin off in the corner. Simply put, the 10 pin is bowling's version of flipping someone the bird. It was a tough break that Schlegel, like most right-handed pro bowlers, had suffered countless times before. Sometimes, even a great shot that properly strikes the pocket and ignites the pin action required to stuff all ten pins in the pit still can leave that corner pin standing. Sometimes the problem is a bad rack of pins, which occurs when a misaligned pinsetter sets a pin or even several pins slightly off their spots. Even if the rack is pristine, the bowling ball sometimes will deflect off of the headpin in a way that causes the 6 pin to twirl around the 10 pin and leave it standing rather than slap it out of the rack for a strike. Such a deflection can be the result of changes to the pattern of oil on the lane that occur as bowlers manipulate the lane pattern; those changes can alter the bowling ball's angle of entry into the pocket, affecting the way the ball moves through the pins to the player's detriment. A legendary pro bowler named Don Johnson famously left the 10 pin in the memorable title match of the 1970 Tournament of Champions on the final shot of what would have been a 300 game worth a bonus check of $10,000. He collapsed to the ground, prostrate and devastated, as his opponent, Rick Ritger, came out on the approach to help him to his feet like a man trying to aid somebody who had just been struck the street.

Fortune had intervened for Pedersen; Schlegel found no such luck. He winced as he returned to wait for his ball to come back, and the microphone pinned to his fuchsia shirt documented his disgust.

"Yeah, you didn't look! Didn't look at that lousy rack, Schlegel!" he fumed in his Manhattan accent. "Why didn't you look first! Ernie, Ernie, geez. You didn't even look at it."

One game of bowling offers ten frames to end up with a better score than the other guy. To blow one of them on a perfect shot is to tempt fate once too often. Schlegel gathered himself and made the spare, then struck again on his next shot. This time, he turned back disgusted, shaking his head, and still ruminating over "that lousy rack" as he took his seat.

Schlegel may have been in his fifties, but the thing about bowling pins is they do not know how old you are. And neither, apparently, did Schlegel.

The camera spotted a rioting fan in the crowd holding up a sign that said "Ernie's Army."

"There's Ernie's Army! You remember Arnie's army! We're in Pennsylvania, not too far from Latrobe!" Anthony said of golfing great Arnold Palmer's hometown in southwest Pennsylvania. "We've got Ernie's army, here in the Pittsburgh area!"

Schlegel stepped up in the seventh frame to the crowd's chants of "Ernie! Ernie!" Pedersen did what he could, but it was Schlegel's hand this crowd was eating from now. He blasted another strike. Durbin joked that Schlegel had "thrown the left jab . . . now he's looking for the right cross." Anthony chuckled. Schlegel delivered the right cross in the eighth frame, another resounding strike that blew the rack of pins violently back into the pit. Then he did it again in the ninth. This time, he trotted back to his seat scowling and pumping a clenched fist. "He's mine! He's mine!" he shouted. The arena's writhing crowd erupted as if they could reach a decibel so high they might steer fate themselves.

The camera panned to Schlegel's wife and now-grown daughter, Cathy and Darlene, who exploded out of their seats in the crowd after his eighth-frame strike. Darlene had flown in the day before to be there.

Professional bowling is a lonely sport. For all the legends who may have left their fingerprints on Schlegel's character back in the days of pre-dawn bets and gangsters, for all the fist pumps fans may perform in unison with him, the only way to win in bowling is to stand on the approach alone and go. First, he had to sit through Pedersen's ninth-frame shot. It was a perfect strike—perhaps his best of the match—after which Pedersen performed his best Hulk Hogan. He cupped his hand to his ear to elicit the crowd's praise as he turned to take his seat. That was the last strike he would throw.

Schlegel stared down the pins through his wide-lens glasses, gulped a mouthful of air and exhaled hard from somewhere deep within himself. Somehow, amid all the frenzy and bombast, his mousy hair still sat neatly parted on his head. The TV lights glimmered off of his receding hairline. He looked down at his ball once more and adjusted his stance slightly, then looked back up at the pins with his mean mouth and narrowing eyes, his gnarled nose still striped with an ivory Breathe Right strip.

"Biggest shot of the match, right here," Anthony said.

And as Schlegel ran to the opposite lane pumping his fist after blasting the pocket yet again for a strike, Anthony asked the question many in the arena surely were pondering by now.

"How can he do it any better than that?" Anthony says. "Fifty-two years old, and he's running them out!"

Schlegel's strike on his last ball in the tenth frame forced Pedersen to strike on his next shot or go home a loser. The cameras caught Pedersen mumbling to himself in his seat as he stared down the ten pins that stood between him and $40,000.

"One shot," he seemed to say to himself. "One time."

The golden smile of the kid from San Marino once known on tour as "Captain Happy" was noticeably missing when Pedersen took the approach. Now he wore the stormy poker face of a man with nothing on his mind but the business before him—throw a strike and sign the back of that $40,000 check. Anything less and you lose.

"Well, it's all up to Randy Pedersen," Anthony said. "One ball, and we'll know if we've got a winner or a loser right here."

Pedersen got the shot off quickly. Anthony had hardly finished that last sentence before the ball was halfway down the lane.

The shot was every bit as perfect as his last three, each of which crunched the pocket for no-doubt strikes.

Pedersen was about to be reminded that in bowling, as in life, sometimes perfect is not good enough.

Seconds after Pedersen got the shot off, he collapsed to the ground in a fetal position. His face turned as red as a beet as he buried it in his hands. Like everyone else in the building, he could not believe what he had just seen. His ball angled violently toward the pocket the way it had so many times before in this game. But this time, a single pin in the back row—the 8 pin—remained standing. In professional bowling, it is a break so devastating it has its own name; pro bowlers call it "the stone 8." The ball cleared the pins off the deck so violently that none remained to give this one the kind of fortuitous nudge from which Pedersen benefited earlier in the game. It was as alone on the pin deck as Pedersen was on the floor, the arena roiling with the screams of a disbelieving crowd.

Schlegel came unhinged.

"I don't believe it! I don't believe it!" he shouted as he lunged out of his chair flailing his fists. "Unbelievable!

Thirty years earlier, in an action match against Mike Limongello, Schlegel needed a strike in the tenth frame to shut out Lemon. He threw a clutch shot that seemed destined to hammer the pocket when Cliff Burgland, another bowler who happened to be betting on Lemon, screamed "somehow!" loud enough to be heard from one end of the bowling alley to another. He knew Schlegel's shot was a strike; he screamed out of a desperate hope that somehow the perfect ball Schlegel had thrown would leave a pin standing. Schlegel's ball plowed through the pocket only to leave the dreaded stone 8 pin, losing the match and lining Burgland's pockets. Schlegel had that match in mind when he watched the ball clear Pedersen's hand in the tenth frame, thirty years from that match with Lemon. He screamed *Somehow!* inside his head. And, somehow, it happened—Pedersen left the very stone 8 that had doomed Schlegel that long-ago night against Lemon. Quite literally, Schlegel could not believe it.

Pedersen gingerly picked himself up off the floor.

"For the old people!" Schlegel screamed. "I am the greatest! Muhammad Ali!"

Later, some would take that reference as an arrogant suggestion that he was Ali's equal; in fact, Schlegel meant it merely as an homage to his idol.

Schlegel continued running from one end of the set to the other, reveling in his glory.

"Well, let's hope Ernie doesn't have any heart problems," Anthony said, "because he is *flying!*"

Schlegel's heart made it through fine. It was Pedersen's heart that broke.

There would be no shortage of opinions about the way Schlegel handled his good fortune that night. Many would say Schlegel could have been more graceful about it, that they themselves never would have reacted that way, that Schlegel should have acknowledged, at least, the great but doomed shot he had thrown in that clutch moment.

Years later, Schlegel had his own take.

"Hey, half a million people may love me, half a million people may hate me, but that's a million people who are gonna watch me.'"

EPILOGUE

first met Ernie Schlegel at a senior pro bowling tournament called the Treasure Coast Open at Stuart Lanes in Stuart, Florida, in January 2007. I went to see the guys I loved to watch on TV when I was a kid. I had no idea Schlegel would be there, and I was thrilled to see that he was. I was also thrilled to see other legends in attendance, including Mark Roth and Johnny Petraglia. Unsurprisingly, both Petraglia and Schlegel made the championship round of the Treasure Coast Open, although neither man went on to win the title that week. That went to another Hall of Famer named Dale Eagle.

As I squeezed my way through the crowd to watch the action, I struck up a conversation with Cathy, still as elegant as ever. I told her how much I enjoyed watching Schlegel bowl on TV when I was a kid. She soon introduced me to the man himself.

He looked right at me and said, "I'm the greatest hustler who ever lived." I expected nothing less. Schlegel did not know then that I grew up watching him on TV. I was mesmerized by his performance on the 1995 Touring Players Championship show, which I watched the day it aired. For months afterward, when I would go bowling with my best friend, Dominic Perri, at Melody Lanes in the Sunset Park area of Brooklyn, I would leap, scream, rant, and rave in the manner of the man who had captured my imagination—Ernie Schlegel.

In March 2009, I headed out to Las Vegas to spend some time with the Schlegels. Ernie planned to attend a fiftieth reunion at the South Point Hotel, Casino and Spa with buddies from the old neighborhood. Vegas remains one of the world's premier destinations for elite bowlers to compete for good money. The city has hosted some of the greatest events in the history of the PBA, such as the Showboat Invitational, the Tournament of Champions, and the World Series of Bowling. As long as its casinos throb with the glittering din of slot machines, the outbursts of gamblers waving fists full of betting sheets at football scores and horses, and the shrieks of players wielding royal flushes at poker tables, it will be the only place on earth where Schlegel and his posse from the old days will want to kick back and remember how it was.

Schlegel and his buddies holed up in a penthouse suite to—what else?—play Texas hold 'em for money. The names of those around the table were not so much the names of people as they were the names of memories—Mickey Kennedy, Jerry Markey, Matty Lynch, Billy Jones, Joey Keane, Mike McKeon, Eddie O'Brien, Danny Breheny, Pat Jacoby, Helayne Van Houten. They all had come to Vegas to see what had become of their old friends since the days when Schlegel was a no-name kid at 42 Sickles Street waiting for his life to begin.

The room's one window stretched from wall to wall and offered a view of wheat-brown mountains and valleys that seemed to stretch to the edge of the world. With its thousands of rooms and abundance of glassy windows that glow like gold in the sun, the South Point is an imposing edifice at the south end of Las Vegas Boulevard—about a $40 cab ride from the action at the heart of town. Its remoteness amid the yawning backdrop of desert that surrounds it casts its gaudy splendor in a particularly absurd light. Few spots in town do more to magnify the artificiality of a vacant desert blemished with that false jewel of a city.

Schlegel and the boys soon had other matters to tend to, matters so pressing they achieved the highly unlikely feat of wrenching these men away from their cards. They headed downstairs to the Silverado Steakhouse, where they lifted their drinks in tribute to the ones who ought to have been there with them.

The Silverado is a slim rung shy of the sort of place where bowtied busboys rush to sweep the tablecloth of crumbs while your Veal Francaise arrives with a side of sautéed morels. As waiters whizzed by in their vests amid a chic ambience of dimmed chandeliers, high-backed booths, and walls lined with murals, Schlegel's lifelong friend, Mickey Kennedy, stood and held his glass in the air.

"To those we lost in Vietnam," Kennedy said, "to those who died too young, to those we loved and did not tell, to those we admired and kept our silence, to all who were part of our lives, we raise our glasses and toast to you."

The restaurant's windows flickered with the glow of lights from nearby slot machines as Kennedy and the gang clinked glasses. A rollicking casino in Vegas may seem like an odd setting for a eulogy, but only to those who were not there for games of high-stakes cards in Schlegel's room or those bad nights of betting against the wrong kind of crowd down in Philly. To remember their fallen friends anywhere else would be to dishonor them.

And anyhow, Schlegel would not have it any other way. He hunted for the first craps table he could find the second he stepped out of the Silverado, raving about the quality of their eggplant parmesan and holding his belly with both hands as if it might burst.

"Every Sunday during football season, Ernie's up in his cave watching the games. He always has a couple of bets, and when he roots and screams the entire house shakes," Cathy told me. "I just go downstairs and try to stay calm."

Schlegel cut through the Del Mar Lounge where smokers twirled their cocktails with cigars pinched between their fingers. He zeroed in on a table. The boxman eyed the chips, the base dealers collected their debts, and the stickman raked in the dice. Just as he did so many times on TV over the years, Schlegel found center stage at the head of the table and performed. The handful of gamblers nursing their Captain & Cokes around the table did not know it yet, but it was time for the Ernie Schlegel Show—and they were the audience.

"Four to one for the poor one, baby!" Schlegel shouted as he took the dice and rattled them in his fists. "I'm on Social Security here, OK? I'm on welfare! Gimme a hard eight!"

His wild, blue eyes almost seemed to tremble in his face like the dice in his hands as he came unhinged. He gritted his teeth and scowled with the look of the Other Ernie. His jowly face may have betrayed his age by then, and his broad-lensed glasses and button-down shirt tucked neatly into his Dockers may have conveyed the image of a docile nine-to-fiver. But even at age sixty-six, there still was something feral in him.

He raved at the head of the table until a few hours shy of sunrise, possessed by the narcotic adrenaline of windowless casinos where time is measured in the number of tugs it takes a slot machine to bleed your pockets dry.

"When I was at the craps table last night it started to feel like the old days," Schlegel told me the next day. "I wanted to jump across the table and snap that guy's neck," referring to a twenty-something wise guy who looked on in displeasure at Schlegel's monopolization of the table.

Just like the old days indeed.

That morning, he headed off to the bowling tournament he had come to compete in, the United States Bowling Congress Open Championships. He promptly dropped $600 cash on "brackets"—a form of side-gambling that pits bowlers in head-to-head against each other. Brackets can net you thousands of dollars if you make your bets wisely and the pins fall your way. Cathy, hearing of the amount that Ernie wagered, looked as though she had swallowed a fly.

"Ladies and gentlemen, we have a very special bowler in our midst this afternoon," a tournament official announced to the crowd, "1996 USBC Masters champion, seven-time PBA titlist and Hall of Famer, Ernie Schlegel!"

Schlegel won that USBC Masters title mere months after becoming the oldest player ever to win a major on the PBA Tour at the 1995 Touring Players Championship. (As of this writing, that record still stands.) By then, John Mazzio had succumbed to heart disease, and Schlegel tearfully dedicated the title to his former mentor during the check and trophy presentation following the title match.

Schlegel took a drawn-out bow with a wave of his hand as the venue erupted with applause, a tuft of thinning, dirty-blond hair falling over his face as he lowered his head. It was the applause he had heard somewhere inside those long-ago dreams of the day he would make it big.

Schlegel may have been in his sixties by then, but it took him only one game to demonstrate that he still had it. He came out steaming and recorded a first game in the 230s—full of the fist pumps and gritted teeth for which he was known.

Shortly before bowling that tournament myself, I practiced with Schlegel. He gave me some tips, particularly on how to properly convert a 10 pin spare. He coached me on how to manipulate my hand position to ensure that any ball I threw would take a direct path to the 10 pin.

"I try to throw it straight, Ernie," I told him. "It's hard sometimes."

"Yeah?" he said. "You ever try to get a hard-on? We don't try; we do."

And so he did. He converted one 10 pin spare after another, often dumping the ball almost at the foul line and throwing it so perfectly straight that it seemed to sail up the first board for nearly the entire sixty feet of the lane to convert the 10 pin. That is incredible precision and control; Schlegel still possessed both in abundance.

Later that year, the Schlegels were kind enough to welcome me into their home in Vancouver for almost a week. I spent that time going to various area bowling alleys with him, meeting various bowlers, and listening to the Schlegels' stories—both Ernie's and Cathy's.

One thing a retired Ernie Schlegel did not need to do was get up early on a Saturday morning to cheer on bowlers at a local youth league, yet that is exactly what he did during my visit. I accompanied him to Allen's Crosley Lanes in Vancouver, where he joined twelve-year-old Takota Smith for a round of practice.

Schlegel was up to his old tricks. He heaved his ball straight up the 7 board and guided it toward the headpin with flailing arms and a swinging fist. As the pocket collapsed for a strike, he turned to Takota and playfully gave him the business.

"I'll squash you like a grape!" he said in his still-potent Manhattan accent. He shared a chuckle with the boy's father, who had also joined the action.

Schlegel had known Takota's stepmother, Autumn, ever since Schlegel roomed with her father on tour decades ago. When Autumn tragically lost both her father and mother, Schlegel took her and her brothers Jeremy and Jason under his wing. Now he had a new "nephew" to mentor—young Takota Smith, whom he recently had introduced to the sport.

"He loves those kids like they are his boys," Cathy told me. "He is Uncle Ernie to them. Jason has a two-year-old now who just goes crazy when she sees him."

That is the Ernie Schlegel people know in Vancouver, not the brash kid from the streets of New York. Now he is the "crazy uncle" who is as sure to show up and watch the Saturday morning youth leagues as the parents of the bowlers themselves.

He is also the grandfather who speaks to his grandson, Zachary Connor, at the same day and time each week by webcam. Amid a recent visit to see his daughter Darlene in Florida on Zachary's birthday, Schlegel quickly found himself coaching youth bowlers at the local bowling alley there.

"I just can't seem to not help kids," Schlegel told me. "You never know who is going to be the next great one."

Schlegel's interest in affecting youth bowlers with the love for bowling he discovered as a kid himself derives from his concern for a sport that once enjoyed a cultural prominence it has lost over the years. The PBA Tour is a shadow of what it was in Schlegel's prime due largely to forces beyond the control of its executives. A tour that once brought action to more than 30 cities throughout the United States over the course of a season now hardly visits a handful. Most events it does put on, such as the World Series of Bowling or the Summer Swing, conglomerate many separate tournaments that run simultaneously under one roof to avoid the production and travel costs incurred by a bonafide tour that takes each tournament to a new town.

Pro bowlers who wish to make a living on the lanes today must consent to be globe-trotters, as competitive bowling increasingly is an international enterprise that takes players everywhere from Russia to Malaysia, Korea to Poland, France to Qatar and all points in between. Those 20 million viewers before whom Schlegel performed on ABC in the mid-1970s have dwindled to as few as 800,000, and the ABC network cancelled its weekly pro bowling telecast after a 35-year run in 1997. Its last show went out with a tearful goodbye from longtime broadcast partners, Chris Schenkel and Bo Burton; their tears reflected the sentiments of many who remembered what once had been.

Major corporate sponsors that once regularly bolstered PBA Tour events, such as Firestone, Quaker State, or Miller Lite, have long since moved on. The loss of those big-time title sponsors, and the PBA's ongoing struggle to attract new ones in an economic climate immeasurably more challenging than it was when TV offered a mere handful of channels rather than the thousands available today, continues to impact the PBA Tour—and the bowling industry at large—with adversities that seem nearly insurmountable at times. In 2014, professional bowling's U.S. Open, an event every bit as prestigious in bowling as it is in golf or tennis that had run annually since 1971, was cancelled. The 2015 event also was cancelled briefly before the event's long-time sponsor, the Bowling Proprietors' Association of America, inked a partnership deal with the United States Bowling Congress, the sport's governing body in the U.S., to keep the event alive for at least a few more years. Budgets throughout the bowling industry are leaner than seemingly ever before; executives and journalists who have worked in bowling for decades openly concede they never have seen things as financially tight as they are today.

None of the PBA Tour's current ills are due to a lack of effort. Its visionary commissioner, Tom Clark, and his veteran team of bowling lifers such as Mike Jakubowski, Kirk Von Krueger,

Dave Schroeder, Jason Thomas, Bill Vint, and Jerry Schneider, among others, continue to battle through grueling circumstances with concepts and programs designed to save costs and turn back at least some of the tide that threatens to submerge professional bowling in the United States. The PBA made its entry into the new media landscape with its subscription-based online streaming product, Xtra Frame, which offers unlimited coverage of live events plus a growing archive of historical content. Clark is the architect of forward-looking concepts such as the World Series of Bowling, which has succeeded in saving costs while providing international players with an unprecedented opportunity to bowl a number of PBA tournaments for a fraction of the cost required in the days when each tour stop was held in a different city. The production of many events and TV show tapings for ESPN in a matter of about ten days requires an ungodly amount of hours from the PBA's limited staff; it is an undertaking that defines the term "labor of love." The current woes faced by the PBA Tour—and by the bowling industry at large—have bred a screaming chorus of critics full of hot air about what went wrong and how it can be fixed. Most critics who insist they have the answers have little idea how much work is going into keeping competitive bowling viable despite the adverse circumstances it faces. If they did, they, too, might consider that a minor miracle.

Clark also succeeded in returning the PBA to its former glory on ABC in 2011, when the storied Tournament of Champions returned to the ABC network with a special appearance by beloved announcer Bo Burton; Chris Schenkel had passed away in 2005 at age 82. That event awarded the richest top prize in PBA Tour history, $250,000, which went to PBA Tour veteran, Mika Koivuniemi. Koivuniemi bowled a 299 in the semifinals of that TV show, falling a pin short of a televised perfect game while his opponent, Tom Daugherty, infamously bowled a score of 100. That outcome marked the greatest discrepancy between two combatants in the history of the PBA Tour's televised finals, and it made for some of the greatest drama in recent pro bowling memory. The show opened with a live performance by punk-pop band, Bowling for Soup, who used the opportunity to introduce their catchy new single, "S-S-S-Saturday," to a national TV audience. On the women's side of professional bowling, the Bowling Proprietors' Association of America has produced the championship finals of the U.S. Women's Open in exotic settings such as outdoors under the arches in Reno on specially constructed lanes or inside the palatial Cowboys AT&T Stadium in Arlington, Texas. Some argue that these one-off events do more to convey desperation than they do to solve the problems pro bowling faces because they do not cultivate a sustained, returning audience. But even critics have to at least admit that these events demonstrate the bowling industry's resolve to never give up at a time when it would be easy to do so.

Perhaps the saddest episode to occur amid the struggles that have dogged professional bowling in recent years was the dissolution of the women's pro bowling tour in 2003 due to financial woes. For more than forty years, the women's pro bowling tour had provided many great female competitors the chance to make a living on the lanes. Even though the women's tour has been defunct for more than a decade now, a crop of phenomenally talented, young women bowlers has emerged at a time when they may never know what it is like to have a tour of their own. When Kelly Kulick became the first woman bowler to win a PBA Tour title after defeating PBA Tour superstar Chris Barnes in the title match of the 2010 Tournament of Champions, the victory did as much to move women's professional athletics forward as it did to highlight the irony that some of the most talented woman bowlers who ever lived have reached their competitive prime at a time when they have little to bowl for.

Ernie Schlegel believes one way to possibly reverse pro bowling's downward trend is to cultivate a new generation of young, passionate and competitive bowlers who can ensure its relevance in the decades to come. He concedes that bowling is the thing that saved his life. His suspicion before Esposito allowed him on tour in 1968 that the life of a bum awaited him was no exercise in paranoid conjecture; it was very real. If bowling can do for any other kid what it did for him in his youth, Schlegel wants to make it happen. It is a difficult endeavor, as competition in the children's sports marketplace is heated. Pop Warner football, little league, soccer, hockey, basketball, lacrosse, martial arts and a host of other activities have combed the ranks of once-flourishing youth bowling leagues and left them with many fewer participants today than they enjoyed even fifteen years ago. Nonetheless, it is a fact that high school bowling ranks among the fastest-growing sports in the United States, and that college bowling, too, is thriving.

The Ernie Schlegel who wakes up early on Saturday mornings to coach youth bowlers may be a softer version of the one who proclaimed himself "The Greatest" on ESPN, but the Other Ernie showed up during my time in Vancouver as well. The day after heading off to Crosley Lanes together, Schlegel bowled a tournament at another local center. He showed up five minutes before the practice session was set to start, and one diminutive, twenty-something bowler made the mistake of saying something.

"Maybe we could actually get some practice if Ernie would show up on time," the kid said loudly enough for everyone to hear.

"Don't make me come down there and make you smaller than you are!" Schlegel shouted. "Guys like you I used to squash and put them in my back pocket. I think I still got one back there."

In case anyone who heard him dared to doubt the truth of what he said, Schlegel rode consecutive 250 games into first place with two games to go in a field of bowlers young enough to be his children.

"I wonder how long he can keep this up?" Cathy said to me as we watched Schlegel compete.

Schlegel placed third and left the place with more cash in his pocket than he had when he arrived. Just like the old days. It seemed clear to me then that he would keep it up for as long as he wanted to.

ACKNOWLEDGMENTS

The writing of this book has been the most challenging thing I ever have done in my life. Years ago, I read something by Norman Mailer in which he described the experience of writing a book as "physically debilitating." I was a kid then afflicted with the unfortunate dream of becoming a writer—a doomed aspiration I wish on no one—and I thought I knew what Mailer was talking about. I did not. Not even close. Writing this book has indeed proven physically debilitating. At times, I felt like the star of the myth of Sisyphus, rolling this boulder uphill only to watch it slide back down and do it all over again. But just as Mike Limongello says he would not trade his memories of the old action days for anything, I myself would not trade an ounce of the sweat I poured into this book for anything. I have made lasting friends who have welcomed me into their homes and treated me as though I were their son, opened their lives to me, and given me so much more than the good stories for which I initially pursued them. My gratitude is boundless.

That I somehow managed to finish this book is a miracle for which I have many people to thank. But there is one person in my life who had to *endure* the writing of this book, and that person is my amazing wife, Brittni. Her patience, support, and understanding got both of us through the most trying moments we experienced together over the past five years. And toward the end of that five-year period, on December 5, 2013, she gave me the greatest gift I ever have received, as our beautiful daughter, Ellianna, was born that day.

As someone who grew up watching Ernie Schlegel bowl on TV as a kid, the fact that I ended up telling his story years later is a twist of fate I never could have foreseen and never will believe. The Schlegels rank among the sources for this book who began as sources and ended up as lifelong friends. Their hospitality, compassion, and friendship throughout the arduous process of this book's creation provided a galvanizing source of fortitude and inspiration over the years.

Steve Harris is a source for this book who quickly turned into something more like a father figure. He is one of the most impressive human beings I ever have encountered. His success in business comes despite never acquiring a college degree. The streets of New York taught him the art of the hustle, and, like many former action bowlers, that was all the learning he needed to live on his own terms. It did not take long for me to realize that he is a guy worth listening to about things well beyond the stories I tell in this book. Harris always eagerly and warmly welcomed my repeated questions over the years—so many of them redundant—and his patience is a big reason why this book even was possible to write.

One of my favorite sources for this book is Toru Nagai. I met Nagai briefly at a diner in Las Vegas in my 2009 trip to see and bowl with Schlegel during his 50-year reunion with cherished friends from the old days. Nagai then was well into his 80s, and he still had all of his faculties about him, including a razor-sharp sense of humor and a precise, vivid memory. Nagai enjoyed ribbing Schlegel as we had lunch. Schlegel is a man who loves to talk. PBA Hall of Famer Barry Asher jokes that when he calls Schlegel, he does not have to say anything. He just listens. That tends to be how it is when talking to Schlegel on the phone; it is one of the man's many peculiar charms. When I met Nagai, he joked that a five minute walk often took an hour with Schlegel, because Schlegel would stop him every few seconds to begin a new line of conversation.

My favorite moment having lunch with Nagai and Schlegel out in Vegas came when I busted out a laptop to show them one of the TV shows on which Schlegel appeared in the 1980s. At one point in the show, after Schlegel had thrown a clutch strike late in a match, the camera panned to Cathy in the crowd. She lunged out of her seat with gritted teeth to pump her fist as her crimson hair roiled over her ivory-white forehead. Schlegel loved it.

"That's my mama!" he said. "Look how *mean* she is!"

About a year-and-a-half after first meeting Schlegel, I found Kenny Barber. I say "found" because Barber was not the kind of guy you looked up in the White Pages; he made sure of that. Over the time I knew him—approximately three years, from early 2009 to late 2011, when he died—I believe he changed his phone number at least a handful of times. That was due partly to an ongoing paranoia that no distance from his past could diminish, and partly to the chorus of bill collectors who blew up his phone on a daily basis.

Schlegel had an old number of Barber's laying around. He gave it to me one day and I dialed. I got an answering machine with no message or greeting. Just a tone and the silence into which I spoke my uncertain inquiry about a guy named Kenny Barber I wanted to talk with, and was the person at this number the man himself? Barber was screening his calls. He must have quickly surmised that I was neither a bill collector nor a gangster looking to settle some long-ago grievance that had gone unresolved, because he rang my phone seconds after I hung it up.

The instant he spoke, I knew it had to be the one and only Kenny Barber. There it was—the Queens accent; the lisping speech that made him sound like he had a mouth half-full of water as he spoke; the ghost of Rodney Dangerfield somewhere off in the distance of his gruff voice. (Barber did a hell of a Dangerfield impression.) It was him; he was still alive. The Rego Park Flash, the clown of Gun Post Lanes, the guy who collected for Crazy Vito. In the flesh. I wanted to know everything, and he was happy to give it to me, so desperate was he by then for somebody to care about who he was, where he had been, and the mess he had made of his life.

That mess comprised stories of New York City pro shops that went belly-up when their shady financiers left him holding the bag, a failed attempt to start over out in L.A. at a place called El Dorado Bowl, bad decisions and the things he would give to take them back. There were stories of defrauded creditors he eluded when he left New York, court dates, and a bitter nostalgia that ached more sorely with each passing year.

A lot of things ached in Barber's life by the time I met him: the cirrhotic liver he described as "ninety percent dead"; the new knees he needed; the carpal tunnel that so many years of bowling brought on; the ex-wife who phoned from jail to berate him for not accepting collect calls from her mother.

I later went to meet him at a McDonald's in Cape Coral, Florida, where he lived at the time. He slammed a battered cardboard box onto the table. I did not yet know it, but this box would haunt me for years to come. He nudged open a single flap to reveal its contents, and the box burst open, pregnant with seemingly every instance in which Barber's name appeared in the local bowling news. At this time, he was 65 years old; he had kept this collection of clippings on hand for nearly half a century.

The Styrofoam cup of coffee he lifted to his mouth cloaked his sun-bronzed face with a flash of steam.

"I can't believe I still have all this!" Barber exclaimed as his jewel-green eyes widened over his treasure. "I haven't looked at this stuff in years!"

Each paper he pulled from the box tugged him a little deeper into a moment in his life when he felt most fully alive. The names he read off of the standings sheets of long-ago tournaments read like the names of hustlers chalking their cues somewhere in the corner of a Jackie Gleason movie—Sis Montovani, Doc Iandoli, Nunzio Morra, Mike Limongello, Vinnie Pantuso. They were names of men who had long since disappeared into their lives.

The one name Barber lingered over more than any other was the name of Ernie Schlegel. Schlegel's achievements taunted Barber. Barber grew up a dreamer, too, when he and Schlegel were kids and the mere mention of money ignited an addiction to adrenaline only gamblers know. Schlegel's dream made it to the Hall of Fame; Barber found his in a box he had not dug into for decades, a wild nest of aging papers that contained the comprehensive detritus of his life.

Barber hardly mentioned his box full of press clippings and tournament standings sheets again. How could I have known that he pushed his life across the table at McDonald's that day because he already was thinking about leaving it behind? In December, 2011, Barber took his own life.

I called him up weeks before then, in November, 2011. Things sounded bad, and I did not know what to do. The last thing I said to him was, "You've got to hang in there for me,

Kenny." I had a feeling that the time when he finally would enjoy the recognition he so desperately craved was coming soon. I had been working feverishly on the research for this book for years. I had no clue whether the book ever would see the light of day—no agent, no editor, no publisher. Nothing but hope and a story I had fallen in love with. By the end of 2011, after having nearly given up, I had a feeling something was going to break soon. A year later, it did. My story, "When Thugs and Hustlers Ruled Dark Alleys," appeared in *The New York Times* in November, 2012, complete with a photo of Barber and some of his stories. Part of me was proud as hell that I was able to get his name out there; the rest of me hated the fact that he never would know it. And now, here he is in this book. I told you so, Kenny.

Things did not turn out for Barber the way he had hoped, but the tremendous success he enjoyed as the owner of many pro shops throughout the New York City area earlier in his life was a testament to something that is true of many former action bowlers. Those among them who went on to successful careers in business—and there are many of them—directly credit their experience in the action as the reason for their success.

One such former action bowler, Bill Markus, moved on to a career in finance when he realized he was not quite good enough to pursue his dream of becoming a professional bowler.

"When I would have big business meetings, people would say to me, 'Isn't that a lot of pressure?' I told them pressure is when you make a five-dollar bet and you only have three dollars in your pocket," Markus told me in a 2013 phone interview.

Harris says he "learned a lot more in the bowling alleys at night" than he ever did in college. "How to negotiate, stamina, acting, humor, strategy, how to read people, the art of risk-taking—I learned it all in the bowling alley."

I once took Barber to see another inimitable source for this book, PBA Hall of Famer Larry Lichstein. I convinced him to accompany me to Lichstein's pro shop at a place called Bowland in Cape Coral and have an impromptu reunion with a fellow action bowling legend. It took some prodding. Barber no longer enjoyed bowling alleys. They reminded him that the one thing he loved as much as playing poker now was the one thing his broken-down body could not do. Nonetheless, he agreed to go to Bowland with me. He burst into Lichstein's shop and immediately rolled out a Rodney Dangerfield impression. He did not even say hello; he launched into clown mode as soon as he sauntered into the shop.

Lichstein was stunned.

"Kenny Barber, Kenny Barber," Lichstein repeated over and over with wide eyes. He looked like he was in a trance, as though he were seeing a ghost. In a way, he was. Barber was the ghost of the way things were.

And there was another thing I couldn't resist: the story of how Lichstein went bald. I told him I had heard the story from Jim Byrnes.

Lichstein forced open a collection of crumpled notes that nested inside a mangled magazine in the drawer of his desk. It was a yellowing copy of *Bowlers Journal* from 1969.

"See that!" Lichstein shouted, the words bursting from his body like little lightning storms as he pointed to his picture on the cover. "Who might *that* be! Oh, that's *me!* I see!"

It was hard not to notice that the photo featured a full head of hair before Lichstein thrashed it violently back into the drawer and slammed it shut with a thunderous bang. He stood up again, folded his arms, turned his head forward to leer at me from under his creased brow, and launched into the tale of how he lost his hair.

"I was not terribly happy that I had lost my money, and I let people know about it. And then Jim Byrnes grabbed me by the arms, picked me up, and shoved me right into the trash bin."

Lichstein, in a rhapsodic frenzy now, slapped his bald and bobbling head with two frantic hands, roaring memories and grudges.

"And there I am, upside-down in a trash bin. And there's puke! And shit! And piss! And I've got all this shit all over my head and it stinks!"

He slowed to an abrupt hush and leaned forward to reveal the top of his head.

"And this is the result," he said as the polished top of his bald and peach-colored head shimmered under the lights of his shop, a vague strip of silver hair running up the center of his skull like a zipper.

Another source for this book whom I also must thank is Clifford Nordquist, otherwise known as A.C. Butch. Butch is one of my favorite people in the world, and his passion and support have been a tremendous help over the years. It takes just a few seconds of viewing one of his many YouTube videos, which he posts under the username "actionbowlers," to determine that Butch is one of Brooklyn's greatest characters. And there are many great characters in Brooklyn. I know; I grew up there. One such video was a tribute to me he produced in 2011. That was an act of kindness I never anticipated and did not ask for. Butch always has surprised and supported me with a generosity, sincerity, and authenticity I rarely encounter. He also is the man behind the great actionbowlers.com website, which is not so much a website as it is an odyssey through a world we cannot have back.

In addition to Butch, the inimitable PBA Hall of Famer, Len Nicholson, has been one of my most ardent supporters over the years. He has graciously provided me with many opportunities to promote this book—and my work as a journalist, poet, and academic—on his internet radio show, Phantom Radio. I never quite know what I am in for any time I get on the phone with Lenny, as anyone lucky enough to also call him a friend knows. And that is just how I like it. Unpredictable, bawdy, hilarious, candid, immensely knowledgeable, competent, sharp—those are just some of the many superlatives I could summon to describe how impressive a man Nicholson is. I am so blessed to call him my friend. Above all, Nicholson cares deeply about the future of the sport he loves—bowling—and he will remain committed to his goal of educating people about where the sport once was, where it is headed, and why, until his last breath. And he is the reason I got the chance to meet and speak with the great Billy Hardwick in the years before his death on November 16, 2013, as Lenny was one of Billy's best friends. May Billy rest in peace.

I must also thank everyone at the Professional Bowlers Association who helped me cultivate an awareness of this book among their fans. In particular, Mike Jakubowski, Bill Vint, Jerry Schneider, Jason Thomas, Jef Godger, Tom Clark, and Dave Schroeder. Additionally, I am grateful for the support I have enjoyed from the good people at *Bowlers Journal International*, including Bob Johnson, Keith Hamilton, and Mike Panozzo. I also am grateful to the United States Bowling Congress for their help securing photos and for affording me the opportunity to share my love of bowling history with their members during my time as the Managing Editor and Features Writer for BOWL.com, USBC's official website. Brock Kowalsky at USBC was especially helpful in securing photos.

Thanks as well to Peter Limongello for helping me maintain contact with his legendary father, Mike Limongello. And to Dominic Perri, my best friend, for being the one person with whom I always could share my obsession with the sport of bowling back when we were kids in Brooklyn and the lanes were all we knew.

Lastly, my agent, Laurie Abkemeier, and my editor and publicist at Pegasus Books, Jessica Case, both had the vision to see this book's potential while others turned it down. They are two of the smartest and hardest-working people I ever have known. With their work ethic and insistence on excellence, they restored some of my faith in humans and they challenged me at every turn to aspire to be great. That is an aspiration I will carry with me for the rest of my life, and I always will have them largely to thank for that. I also know that I am a better writer today than I was before I met them; their vision and editorial guidance made that possible. Laurie, in particular, helped cure me of my peculiar affection for coordinating conjunctions and literary sentences that often got in their own way. Laurie helped me discover and unleash the power of simplicity and directness, an aesthetic that will remain a part of my work for years to come.

NOTES

CHAPTER ONE
A FISH IN PHILADELPHIA

The material on Jimmy Dykes at the start of this chapter is well-known, but my particular source for this information was an obituary that appeared in the June 16, 1976 edition of the *Daytona Beach Morning Journal*. The allusion to Minsky's Burlesque and Tempest Storm is drawn from interviews with Steve Harris and from a May 18, 2008 *New York Times* story, "The Almost Naked City," by Mark Caldwell.

Much of the information this chapter presents regarding the origins and history of the sport of bowling derives from two of the greatest bowling history books ever published: Herm Weiskopf's *The Perfect Game* and Mark Miller's *Bowling*. I had the joy of working with Mark during my time at the United States Bowling Congress; the man is a walking encyclopedia of bowling knowledge and a true bowling lifer.

This chapter's recounting of the night Harris, Schlegel and Nagai got a lot more than they bargained for down in south

Jersey derives from interviews I conducted both by phone and in person with Steve Harris, Ernie Schlegel, and Toru Nagai. While Nagai's memory is remarkably clear for a man in his 80s—he recounted in vivid detail how he escaped those south Jersey hoods with Harris and Schlegel in his black Cadillac— Steve Harris is gifted with a photographic memory. Over the years I kept going back to Harris to check my facts and ask him to tell me the story of what happened down at Federal Lanes one more time, and then one more time again, and then again. Every time the details were precisely the same, and every time I would become a little more confident in my ability to tell the story as vividly as he experienced it. It is probably one of my favorite action stories, and I am saying that as someone who has heard more of them than I now can count on twelve hands.

Other sources for this chapter include interviews I conducted with Jim Byrnes, Johnny Campbell and Don Sylvia in Port St. Lucie, Florida in 2009; a phone interview with Sam Taylor, one of Schlegel's earliest sponsors, also in 2009; and interviews by phone and in-person with Kenny Barber, whom I met on several occasions in Cape Coral and in Tampa, Florida from 2009-2011.

CHAPTER TWO
THE GUNS OF AVENUE M

The story this chapter tells about the night a loan shark raised his gun at Avenue M Bowl in Brooklyn derives principally from telephone interviews I conducted with Johnny Petraglia, Mike McGrath, and Richie Hornreich. I had first heard of the story from Barry Asher, who, like Petraglia and McGrath, is a PBA Hall of Famer. He referred me to Petraglia for the rest of the story, as Asher is a west-coast guy out in California who was not present when this incident went down at Avenue M Bowl all those years ago. He and others have told me that Petraglia tells the story best after a few glasses of wine. I was not able to feed Petraglia any wine while speaking with him—that is the downside of telephone communication—but he did still tell a hell of a story. After speaking with him, I moved on to McGrath and Hornreich. A box full of news clippings left to me by Kenny Barber before his death in 2011 also contributed to the names and places I identify in this chapter.

I largely have Clifford Nordquist, who goes by the moniker A.C. Butch, to thank for this chapter's descriptions of Avenue M Bowl. That place was one of Butch's main haunts during his time as a young action bowler in the 1960s. Those who enjoy the stories I tell in this book should treat themselves to Butch's many YouTube videos describing his experiences in the action as a kid and, later, during his mid-1970s "comeback." He posts his videos under the youtube username "actionbowlers."

All the aforementioned names contributed in part to this chapter's recounting of the Iggy Russo story, which is probably the most notorious incident in action bowling lore. I could not speak to any of them without at least some mention of the Russo incident coming up. I also got some information about Russo from phone interviews with Mike Limongello, Jeff Kitter, Lenny Dwoskin, Jack Clemente, Larry Lichstein, Dewey Blair, Red Bassett, Steve Harris, and Ernie Schlegel.

CHAPTER THREE
CENTRAL

While much of the information about Gun Post Lanes and Central Lanes in this chapter comes from the countless hours of interviews I have done with Schlegel and Harris, it also came up in conversations I have had with everyone from big-name players like Petraglia and Limongello to lesser-known, but equally fascinating, figures such as Red Bassett, Dewey Blair, John Kourabas, and Pete Mylenki.

Harris told me the story of poor Checkbook Al, the out-of-luck loser who came around bumming guys at the Central lanes coffee counter for enough money to please Max the Shylock's goons, only to be hurled through a plate-glass window by one of them. Both Schlegel and Harris helped me envision what "Maxie" looked like and sounded like. The story of the match between Lichstein and Barber first came to me from Lichstein himself, who very proudly boasted of the accomplishment when I first went to visit him at his pro shop in Cape Coral, Florida, at a place called Bowland. I figured the best source with whom to corroborate the story would be the person at the worse end of its stick—Kenny Barber. Barber happened to be living in the Cape Coral area, as well, and he corroborated the story in the only way he knew how: "That *fuck* had never bowled that good in his life!" he said. Even fifty years later, Barber still smarted after the beating Lichstein handed him that night at Central. Aside from interviews with Barber himself and the box stuffed with news clippings and family correspondence he left to me, Jim Kaull's April, 1963 piece for *Bowlers Journal International*, "The Restless One," also helped with this chapter's material on Barber. That was one of hundreds of news clippings I found in the box Barber left me.

Lichstein also is the man whose recollections of the night he first met Schlegel inform this chapter's account of the kind of character Schlegel had become by then. Lichstein, like Harris, has an incredibly vivid memory. He remembers specific dates down to the day and scores he and others bowled more than half a century ago in matches few people alive still recall. I often say that the 1960s action bowling scene and the bygone world that made it possible was a time and place when guys like Schlegel, Barber, Lichstein, Harris, Limongello, Hornreich, and so many others felt most fully alive. The rich detail with which Lichstein recorded those days onto the tape recorder of his mind is a testament to just how deeply he savored the life he lived back then.

This chapter's discussion of the doomed National Bowling League stems from a variety of sources. They include two books: *Bowling: America's Greatest Indoor Pastime* by Mark Miller and *The Perfect Game* by Herm Weiskopf. Additional sources include an October, 1961 story in *Sports Illustrated* titled "Bowling's Big League—A $14 Million Gamble"; a story by Ed Piel titled "The National Bowling League Ahead of its Time?" for a regional bowling news publication out of the northwest U.S. called *The Van-Port*; and a February 22, 1984 *New York Times* story by Peter Applebome called "Wide Open Spaces of Texas—Indoors."

The material about Buzz Fazio derives from a February, 1964 story by Steve Cruchon called "Bowling's Indomitable Grandfather," and a May, 2006 story by J.R. Schmidt titled "The Friendly Fire of Fazio," both written for *Bowlers Journal International*. I also used a May, 1957 story by Bruce Pluckhahn titled "Buzz Fazio Decides Future Lies Elsewhere," written for the now-defunct magazine, *Bowling*. Interviews with PBA Hall of Famer Len Nicholson also contributed to this portion of the chapter.

CHAPTER FOUR
THE ROAD TO BUFFALO

The information about the period in his life that Schlegel describes as his "bum period"—that time in the streets in which he endured the lamentable purgatory between his dreams of going pro and Frank Esposito's opposition—comes largely from my interviews with Schlegel himself. I also benefitted from interviews with Pete Mylenki, whom Schlegel credits as the man who saved his life. Mylenki gave me plenty of good information about how far Schlegel had fallen in his life at that time—Schlegel then believed a bum was all he ever would be—but when it came to what Mylenki described as "the dirty details," he directed me to Schlegel. Additionally, I interviewed Schlegel's longtime friends, Steve Harris, Jerry Markey, Mike McKeean, Mickey Kennedy, Matty Lynch, Billy Jones, Joey Keane, Eddie O'Brien, Danny Breheny, Pat Jacoby, Helayne Van Houten, and Sam Taylor.

This chapter's account of the 1969 Greater Buffalo Open mingles the recollections Schlegel shared with me and my own observations upon watching a DVD copy of that show, which I acquired from the PBA. Additionally, PBA.com, the official website of the Professional Bowlers Association, contains an extensive, historical archive chronicling the results of PBA tournaments going back to 1959. It is one of the world's greatest resources for professional bowling history. I regularly combed over that source over the years for information on where Schlegel and others placed in various tournaments throughout the decades, including the 1969 Greater Buffalo Open.

CHAPTER FIVE
THE BICENTENNIAL KID

In addition to many hours of interviews with the Schlegels— both Cathy and Ernie—I drew upon a variety of sources to stitch together this chapter's glimpse into the most colorful moment in Schlegel's professional bowling career. The Schlegels provided me with many pages of archival stories that appeared in magazines and newspapers in the 1970s and '80s. I found many allusions to—and some more involved examinations of—Schlegel's "Bicentennial Kid" days in those stories. They include E.J. Kahn III's profile of Schlegel in a 1976 issue of the now-defunct magazine, *Oui*; and several stories from back issues of *Bowlers Journal International*, including an interview with Schlegel in February, 1997 on the heels of his induction into the United States Bowling Congress and Professional Bowlers Association Halls of Fame, an October, 1975 piece called "Ernie Schlegel, U.S.A., is the Bicentennial Kid" by Jim Dressel, and a February, 1979 story called "The New Testament and Old Wounds of Ernie Schlegel." Other stories that helped lend some perspective to the significance and controversy of Schlegel's daring garb on the PBA Tour included a February, 1979 Dick Evans piece for the *Miami Herald* called "Schlegel Giving Bowling a Needed Injection of Flair," a 1977 story by Chuck Frank called "Outspoken Bowler Schlegel: Mr. USA Does it His Way" that appeared in the *Suburban Tribune*, and a March, 1982 story Herm Weiskopf produced for *Sports Illustrated* called "Licorice Out, Snails In."

This chapter's information about Billy Hardwick, Bobby Jacks and Curt Schmidt derives from interviews with Len Nicholson, Larry Lichstein, Curt Schmidt, Billy Hardwick, Nelson Burton Jr., and, of course, Ernie Schlegel. Additionally, the following stories also helped: an August 7, 2005 story by Mike Henry for *The Bradenton Herald* titled "The Billy Hardwick Story: Tragedy and Triumph"; an August, 1964 story by Dick Denny titled "The Boy with the Golden Claw," an August, 1976 story by Jim Dressel titled "Billy Grows Up," a December, 1986 story by Lynda Collins titled "The Trials of Bobby Jacks," and a November, 1983 story titled "Whatever Happened to Curt Schmidt?" all written for *Bowlers Journal International*; and a June, 1985 story by Wayne Raguse titled "Schmidt 'Pitched' the Pins Over" that appeared in *Bowling Digest*.

CHAPTER 6
THE GORILLAS OF VANCOUVER

This chapter's stories about Gehrmann's gorillas derive from in-person interviews I conducted with Gery Gehrmann and

Schlegel during a 2009 visit to Vancouver. Schlegel and I met up with Gehrmann at a local bagel shop, where Gehrmann emerged out of the fog like some unsteady vessel and entered through glass double doors that almost seemed too narrow to allow his passage. He waved a leathery hand the size of a catcher's mitt in recognition of Schlegel. The paper cup he grabbed to fill with coffee reduced to the size of a kiwi in his grip. Anytime Schlegel complained about the grueling nature of the training regimen to which Gehrmann subjected him, Gehrmann would flash Schlegel a look with those beady blue eyes of his and say "I had no sympathy for you then, and I have no sympathy for you now."

This chapter's recollections of the 1979 Dutch Masters Open rely on interviews with Schlegel and my observations on a DVD copy of the show I obtained from bowling superfan Keith Kingston. Kingston frequented the now-defunct PBA.com message boards, where I connected with him after hearing he had an extensive collection of archival PBA footage he had recorded over the years. I asked him to send me any recordings of PBA shows on which Schlegel had appeared and he was kind enough to send me the 1979 Dutch Masters Open along with several other shows from the 1970s, '80s and '90s.

Other sources for this chapter were Larry Lichstein's November, 1978 story for *Bowlers Journal International*, "The Greatest Non-Champion"; Barry McDermott's December, 1978 story for *Sports Illustrated*, "Their Prix was 10 Grand"; Jack Rux's January 23, 1979 *Oakland Tribune* story, "PBA Cramps Schlegel's Style"; and an undated story Chuck Pezzano wrote for *Bowling* magazine titled "Take it from the Pros."

The material about Mark Roth in this chapter comes from interviews with Mark Roth, Ernie and Cathy Schlegel, and Teata Semiz. Also helpful were PBA.com's online archives, and a July 18, 2004 story by Martin Fennelly for the *Tampa Tribune* called "A Legend in the House."

CHAPTER SEVEN
SHRUGGING OFF THE MONKEY

This chapter's account of the legendary career of Nelson Burton Jr. and the first PBA Tour title Schlegel won at his expense were gleaned from my interviews with Burton and Schlegel, a copy of the 1980 King Louie Open show sent to me by Kingston, stories from back issues of *Bowlers Journal International*, and PBA.com's extensive online archive of past PBA Tour events. I combed over that archive to read about each of the 18 tournaments Burton won in his competitive career, and each helped me unpeel another layer of the man—both as a bowler and as an announcer. *Bowlers Journal International* stories I found particularly helpful in understanding Burton included an April, 1972 story by Don Snyder called "A Portrait of Determination," a November, 1965 piece by John J. Archibald titled "A Chip off a Splendid Block," and a January, 1986 story by Dan Herbst called "Is an Emmy Next for Bowling's Bo?"

Aside from reading up on Burton, I also had the chance to get to know him a bit myself. I happened to bowl league for a couple years at Stuart Lanes in Stuart, Florida, where I moved after obtaining an MFA in creative writing at The New School in New York City. One day, while practicing at Stuart Lanes, I noticed a guy who looked an awful lot like Burton down on lane three shooting some games with his buddies. I walked up to the woman at the front desk and asked who he was; she confirmed my suspicions. I watched him cruise to a practice score of 264, his arm swing smooth as a mirror. At the time, which was 2004, Burton still maintained a 238 average and had the league's high series, an

804. In January of 2014, at age 71, Burton broke the record for three-game series in the Friday Morning Match Play League at Jensen Beach Bowl in Jensen Beach, a small town neighboring Stuart. He bowled games of 300, 288 and 290— an 878 series. Obviously, the man still has game.

CHAPTER EIGHT
THE LAST GREAT ACTION MATCH

I have had the opportunity to speak with Randy Pedersen on a number of occasions. I interviewed him for *Bowers Journal Interactive* in 2013, and I nominated him for the United States Bowling Congress Hall of Fame that same year. The 1995 Touring Players Championship is not an event one just casually discusses with Pedersen. On the rare occasion when that topic did come up between us, I learned that the way things went down that day still irk him to this moment. An October, 1987 *Bowling Digest* story by John J. Archibald titled "A Mature Winner," a May, 1986 story by Bob Johnson titled "The Secret Behind Randy's Work Ethic" and an April, 1989 interview titled "The Amazing Adventures of Captain Happy," all produced for *Bowlers Journal International*, also contributed to this chapter's material on Randy Pedersen. The PBA's online archives also yielded a lot of information about Pedersen as a bowler and as a man.

The 1995 Touring Players Championship is freely available to view on YouTube. I have watched it probably close to 100 times; I first saw it live the day it aired on ESPN. My interviews with Schlegel added valuable context and insight to the show, enabling me to watch it with new eyes so many years after I saw it for the first time. In addition to watching the show and talking about it with Schlegel, PBA.com's online archive and stories sent to me by the Schlegels also helped a great deal.

This chapter's accounts of the televised championship rounds on which Schlegel appeared in the 1980s derive from PBA.com's online archives and YouTube videos of those shows. Interviews with the Schlegels contributed to the material on John Mazzio. Additionally, a July, 1978 story for *Bowlers Journal International by Jim Dressel, "Shrink to the Stars,"* also helped. The stories about evolutions in bowling ball technology, and the machinations pros indulged to manipulate their performance, derive from interviews with Len Nicholson, Larry Lichstein, Ernie Schlegel and PBA.com's online archives.

ABOUT THE AUTHOR

Manzione is one of the world's foremost action bowling historians, and a lifelong bowler himself. He has written on the subject of bowling for all of the bowling industry's highest-profile publications, including BOWL.com, PBA. com, *Bowlers Journal International*, *Bowling This Month*, and *Bowling Digital*. His writing also has appeared in *The New York Times*, *The Paris Review*, *The Southern Review*, *The Southeast Review*, and many other publications. In 2004, he obtained and MFA in creative writing with a concentration in poetry at The New School in New York City. His first book, *This Brevity*, was a poetry collection published by Parsifal Press in 2006. He currently is Editor of *Bowlers Journal International*, the oldest monthly sports magazine in the country. Previously, Manzione taught English and creative writing at the College of Central Florida, the University of Tampa and the University of South Florida. He lives near Tampa with his wife, Brittni, and his daughter, Ellianna.